MY FRIENDS."

JOHN 15:15

**Merry Christmas 2017
from Bethel Baptist's
Children's Church!**

TO:

FROM:

DATE:

FRIENDS WITH GOD

STORY BIBLE

Why God Loves People Like Me

Written by Jeff White

Illustrated by David Harrington

LIFETREE

Group

MyLifetree.com

LIFETREE KIDS

Visit **MyLifetree.com/Kids** for more fun, faith-building stuff for kids!

Friends With God Story Bible: Why God Loves People Like Me

Credits

Author:	Jeff White
Editor:	Jan Kershner
Illustrator:	David Harrington
Chief Creative Officer:	Joani Schultz
Creative Director:	Michael Paustian
Lead Designer:	Stephen Caine
Assistant Editor:	Becky Helzer

PRINT ISBN 978-1-4707-4861-6 | EPUB ISBN 978-1-4707-5015-2
10 9 8 7 6 5 4 3 2 1   25 24 23 22 21 20 19 18 17

Printed in Malaysia.
001 MALAYSIA 0617

DEDICATION

Thank you to all the Sunday school teachers who made Bible stories come alive to me as a kid. I still remember.

Thanks to the world's greatest team: David Harrington, Jan Kershner, Michael Paustian, Stephen Caine, and Joani Schultz. You're the reasons this book is so amazing.

And thank you most of all to those I love the most: my wife, Amy, and my kids, Luke, Daisy, and Cooper. You give me my words and leave me speechless all at the same time.

J.W.

I want to thank my Lord and Savior Jesus for his love and grace and for allowing me to work on this book, which has been a labor of love.

To my beautiful wife, Sidney, and our wonderful children, Chase, Nick, and Emma: I love you more than I could ever express in words.

D.H.

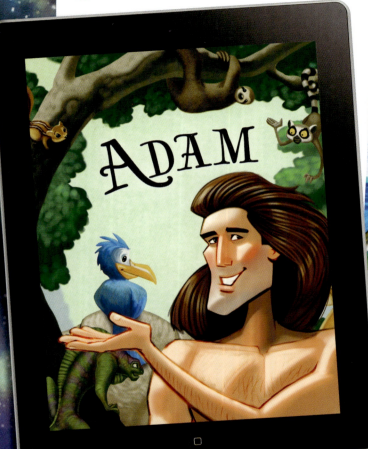

Adam

Best known for:
Being the first human

Hometown:
Garden of Eden

Job:
Animal namer

Favorite food:
Definitely NOT fruit

Friend of God connection: The name Adam means "man." Just like the first Adam, we all have a physical human body. And because of Jesus, we have a spiritual body, too. That's why Jesus was sometimes called the "last Adam."

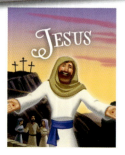

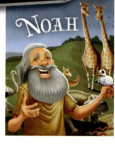

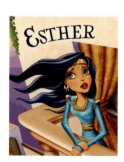

FREE Friends With God App!

Come face to face with Bible-times friends of God. Scattered throughout the pages of the *Friends With God Story Bible*, digital triggers unlock mobile games so you can win virtual collectible cards with entertaining facts about Bible characters. Plus, you'll get a devotional card with a fun idea you can talk about with your family.

▶ Get started in three easy steps:

1. With your parents' help, download the free app available in iTunes and Google Play.

2. When you see this icon 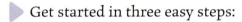, scan the page with your mobile device.

3. Play the games to win all of the collectible cards!

4. Visit **MyLifetree.com/Kids** for more fun, faith-building stuff for kids!

INTRODUCTION

Y ou've never seen a story Bible quite like this one. It has the classic narratives we've all come to know and love over the years: Noah's ark, Joshua and the battle of Jericho, Esther saving her people, and so many more.

But this book is different.

Every story is told from the perspective of a Bible character. Eve tells us what it was like to be tempted in the Garden of Eden. Moses talks about his nail-biting escape from Egypt and parting the Red Sea. We feel David's confidence up close as he recalls facing down one of the biggest bullies of all time.

Yet these first-person chats aren't the only thing that makes this book special. Every story reveals **God's personal relationship with people**. We get straight to the heart of each person and see firsthand how each of their lives changed through their friendship with God.

And at the end of each chapter you'll have a **face-to-face encounter** with the storyteller. He or she will reveal how God was at the center of the story, as well as how it relates to your life today.

Best of all, the *Friends With God Story Bible* will help you dig deep into what faith is really all about: **a one-on-one relationship with the One who loves you the most**.

So circle up your family and get ready to encounter God— and his beloved friends—like never before.

FRIENDS
WITH
GOD
STORY BIBLE

Why God Loves People Like Me

CONTENTS

WOW!
JUST, WOW!
THE DAY GOD MADE ME

GENESIS 1–2:24

BY ADAM

W^{OW}.

I mean, *WOW!*

I can't believe what happened to me today.

I was *created*. And it was AMAZING!

God had been very busy the last few days. First there was nothing. Then every day God made something new. Light, the ocean, the sky, the sun and moon, plants, trees, flowers, fish, birds—you name it. Everything was made for a reason, and it was good.

Yesterday God made these things called animals. They're wonderful creatures! Big ones and small ones. Furry ones and tough ones. Spotted ones and striped ones. Some have long necks, others have sharp teeth. Each one is unique. God is so creative!

15

AND then God made something extra special. God made ME. God took some dirt from the ground—the freshest dirt you've ever seen—and shaped me into the first-ever, brand-new, pleased-to-meet-you human being!

God's world is awesome. I love breathing the crisp air and eating the delicious fruit in the garden. But the thing I love most is what God made just for me.

First, God made me go to sleep. Then God took one of my ribs and turned it into the most dazzling creature I've ever seen: a woman!

She's beautiful! And now she's my wife. We watch over the animals and take care of the garden we live in—the Garden of Eden—together. God has given us everything we need.

God must *really* love us.

Wow!

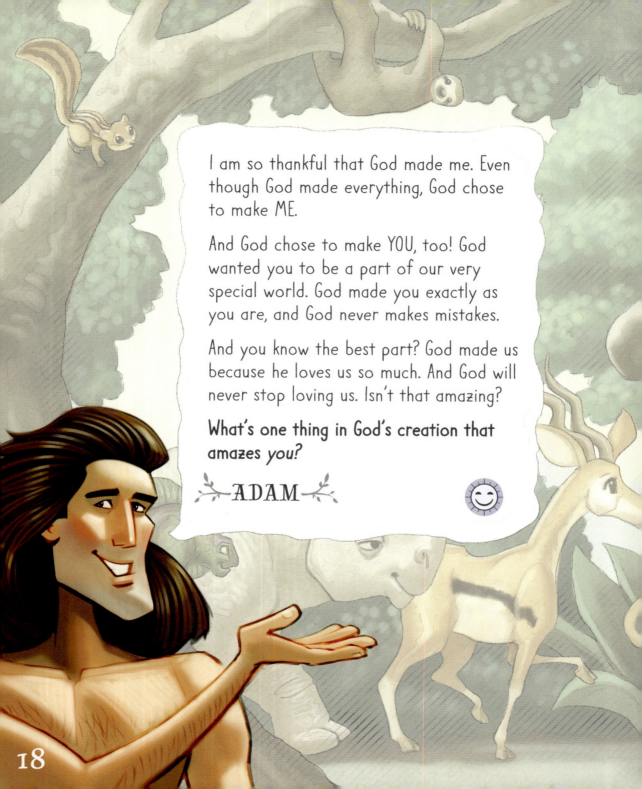

I am so thankful that God made me. Even though God made everything, God chose to make ME.

And God chose to make YOU, too! God wanted you to be a part of our very special world. God made you exactly as you are, and God never makes mistakes.

And you know the best part? God made us because he loves us so much. And God will never stop loving us. Isn't that amazing?

What's one thing in God's creation that amazes *you?*

ADAM

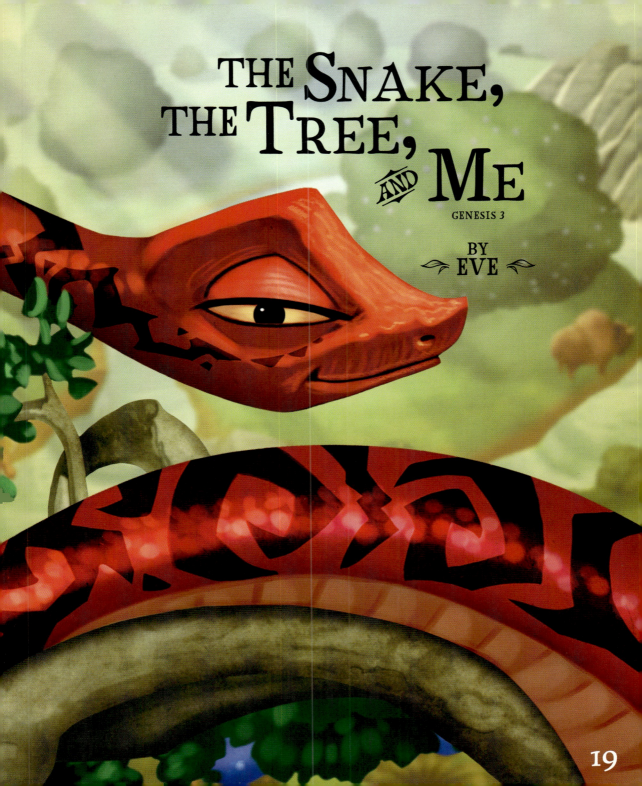

THE SNAKE, THE TREE, AND ME

GENESIS 3

BY ⧼ EVE ⧽

19

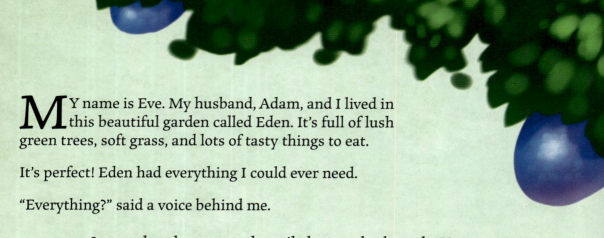

MY name is Eve. My husband, Adam, and I lived in this beautiful garden called Eden. It's full of lush green trees, soft grass, and lots of tasty things to eat.

It's perfect! Eden had everything I could ever need.

"Everything?" said a voice behind me.

I turned and saw a snake coiled around a branch. He was a handsome creature with sharp eyes. He looked very smart.

"Pardon me for interrupting," said the snake, "but you don't have *everything* you could ever want."

I said, "I have a soft place to sleep, a man who loves me, and I never go hungry. God has given me everything I need."

"What about the big fruit tree in the middle of the garden?" the snake asked.

I got a little knot in my stomach thinking about that tree. "God said if we eat that fruit, we'll die," I said.

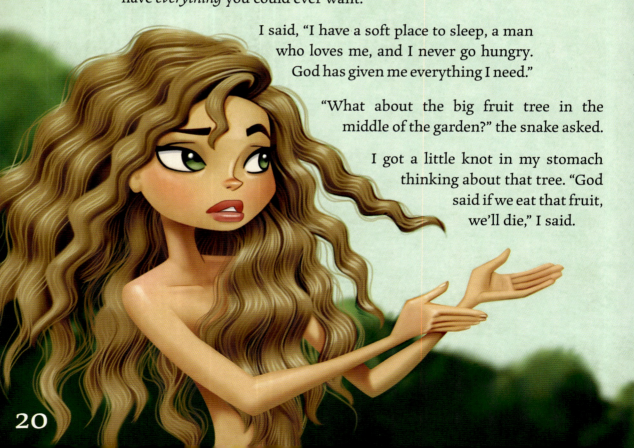

The snake laughed. Then he slithered closer and whispered, "That's silly. God knows you won't die. He also knows it's the best fruit in the garden."

The best fruit? I wondered. "Is that true?"

"Oh, yes. God didn't tell you the special secret about that tree. If you eat its fruit, you'll see amazing things! You'll be able to tell good from evil, just like God himself! Wouldn't it be wonderful to be like God?" said the snake.

Wow, I thought. *God is super powerful. And he's very wise.* I wanted to be wise and powerful just like God. And that fruit *did* look delicious. It made my mouth water just thinking about it.

"How about one little bite?" hissed the snake. "Just a taste. The choice is yours."

I couldn't take my eyes off of that tree. If I didn't try that fruit, I wouldn't be able to think about anything else for the rest of my life.

So I took some of the fruit and had a bite. Mmmmm. It was SO GOOD!

I called to my husband. "Adam! You have to try this!"

"What is it?"

"It's the fruit from the tree in the middle of the garden. It's the best thing I ever tasted!" I told him.

"But isn't that the tree we're not supposed to eat from?" Adam asked, looking around nervously.

"I took a bite, and I didn't die!" I said.

So Adam closed his eyes and took a bite, too. I couldn't wait for his reaction.

But when Adam opened his eyes, he looked afraid. He covered his face and tried to hide. In an instant, we both knew we had made the wrong choice. We felt so ashamed.

After that, God kicked us out of his beautiful garden. Even though God still cared about us, our life got really, really hard. I sure wish I had made the right choice and obeyed God.

I am so ashamed. I had everything going for me, and I blew it. I can't blame the snake. Not really. God had told me what was right and wrong, but I thought I knew better.

Sometimes our choices are fun and easy. But sometimes making the right choice *isn't* easy. I learned that the hard way.

Thankfully, God still loves me anyway. In spite of our wrong choices, God's love for us never stops.

How about you? When have *you* made a bad choice? What happened? How would things have been different if you'd made the right choice?

❧ EVE ☙

24

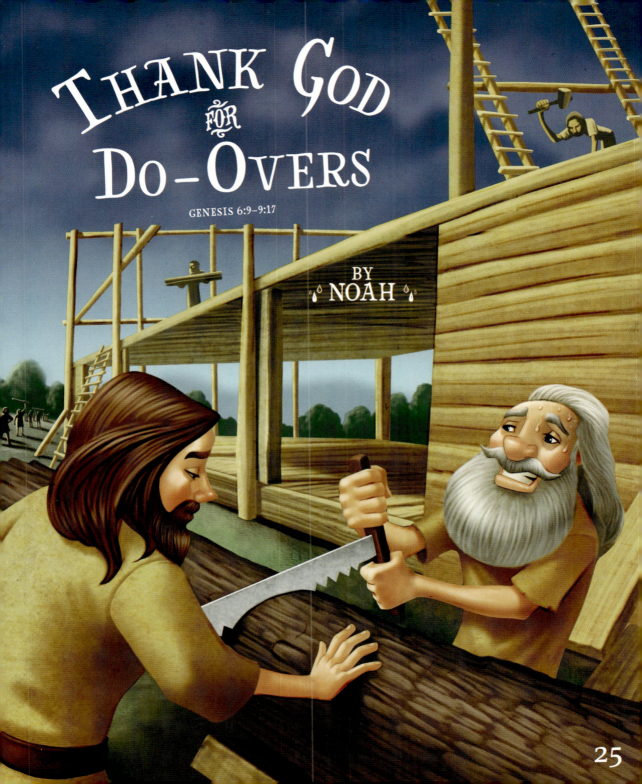

THANK GOD
FOR
DO-OVERS

GENESIS 6:9–9:17

BY
NOAH

25

I like water as much as the next guy. It tastes good. It's refreshing. It keeps my plants green and my body clean.

But man, oh man, there was a time I had WAY TOO MUCH water in my life.

You see, God told me he was unhappy. VERY unhappy. The people of the world had become rather...naughty. Actually, they were awful. They were violent and wicked. And God had had enough.

26

So God told me to build a boat.

"A boat?" I asked. "I don't even live near the water."

"I'll take care of that," God said. "I'm going to destroy every living thing on earth. But since you're a good man, I'm going to save you and your family."

God didn't have to tell me twice. I got busy on that boat right away. My three sons, Shem, Ham, and Japheth, helped, too.

It was a HUGE boat—big enough to be the largest zoo in the history of ever. God wanted me to bring along two of every kind of animal and bird, as well as enough food to feed them and my family. (We left the fish—they didn't mind the extra moisture.)

Then it rained. HARD. And it didn't stop for forty days and forty nights. When the storm was over, the entire planet was flooded.

Eventually the water began to drop, and finally the boat came to rest on a mountain. We had floated around for more than a year. It felt so good to get out of the boat and stretch our legs on dry land again!

But what felt even better was knowing that God had given the world a second chance. Even though God wanted to start over, God still loved us. Now my family can rebuild our world and honor God in all we do. God gave us all a do-over.

So that's me: Noah. Family man. Boat builder. Zookeeper. And most importantly, friend of God.

You might think I've had more than enough water in my life. But God made water to do lots of good things, too. Water gives life to all living things.

God's like that, too. God can clean all the bad stuff out of our lives. And God fills our lives with plenty of good stuff, too.

God even made a promise to never flood the earth again. The rainbow is a sign of that promise, and it reminds us that God loves us and gives us do-overs.

Have *you* ever been given a second chance? How did it make you feel to put your mistakes behind you and start over again?

NOAH

Stars in My Eyes

My Eyes

GENESIS 15

BY
• ABRAM •

THERE are promises, and then there are PROMISES.

God made me a promise that was so hard to believe I just HAD to believe it.

It started when I was feeling sorry for myself. Even though God had blessed me with riches and a long life, even though I'd won battles and made a lot of friends, and even though God had protected me more times than I could count, I was still sad.

I was sad because God hadn't given me any children with my beloved wife, Sarai. How could God bless me with so much, yet not give me a family to share with her?

You know what God did? God made me a promise.

First we went outside, and God showed me the stars in the vast night sky.

"How many stars do you see?" God asked me.

"There are too many to count!" I said.

33

"THAT'S how many descendants you will have," God said. "That's a promise."

Wow. I thought. *That many generations from me?* That's a pretty big family...a HUGE family! I knew God loved me, so I believed him.

But God didn't stop there.

"Your family will need a place to live, so I'm giving you all the land you see before you," God said.

Again, *WOW*.

One thing's for sure. I'll never look at the stars the same way again.

I think there's something really interesting about God's promises. They often come when we least expect it. Just when everything seems hopeless, God comes through with a promise to take care of us.

That's what friends do. I should know, because people call me a "friend of God."

God is your friend, too. When you pay attention to God's words, you can hear many of God's promises to you. And the biggest one of all is that God will always love you.

Have *you* ever made a promise to someone? What was it? Was it easy or hard to keep your promise? When God makes a promise, he ALWAYS keeps it!

ABRAM

Laughing Matters

GENESIS 18:1-15; 21:1-6

BY ❧ SARAH ❧

I'VE seen a lot of funny things in my old age, but I've never laughed as hard as I did today.

It started when I saw my husband, Abraham, talking to some strangers outside. They must have been pretty important men because Abraham served them a fancy meal of roasted meat, bread, yogurt, and milk.

While they were talking, I heard one of them say, "When I come back next year, your wife, Sarah, will have a son!"

Ha! I laughed to myself. *Abraham and I are too old to have kids! We should be grandparents by now, but it's too late for us.*

But the men happened to be from God. Oops! They heard me.

"Don't laugh," the Lord said. "Nothing is too hard for God."

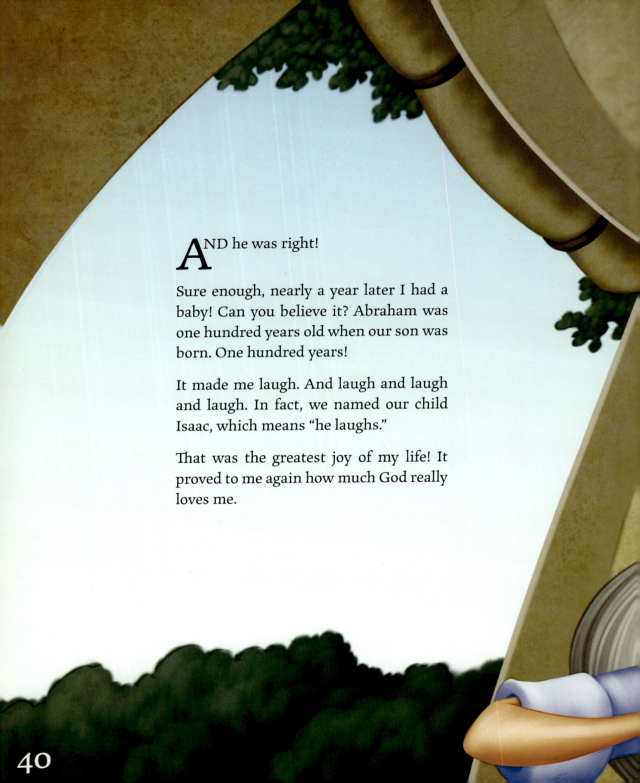

AND he was right!

Sure enough, nearly a year later I had a baby! Can you believe it? Abraham was one hundred years old when our son was born. One hundred years!

It made me laugh. And laugh and laugh and laugh. In fact, we named our child Isaac, which means "he laughs."

That was the greatest joy of my life! It proved to me again how much God really loves me.

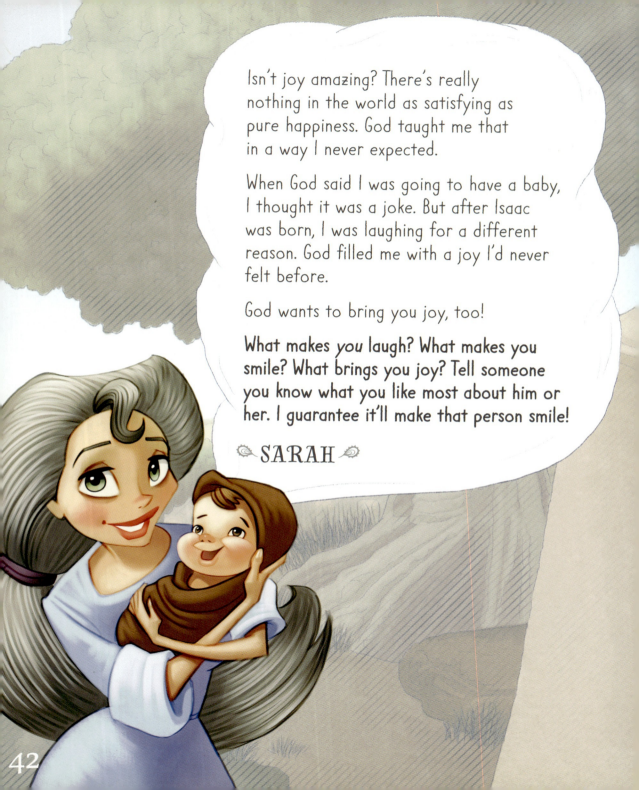

Isn't joy amazing? There's really nothing in the world as satisfying as pure happiness. God taught me that in a way I never expected.

When God said I was going to have a baby, I thought it was a joke. But after Isaac was born, I was laughing for a different reason. God filled me with a joy I'd never felt before.

God wants to bring you joy, too!

What makes *you* laugh? What makes you smile? What brings you joy? Tell someone you know what you like most about him or her. I guarantee it'll make that person smile!

❧ SARAH ❧

A SURPRISE ENDING

GENESIS 27; 32–33

BY JACOB

I hate to admit it, but sometimes I'm not the nicest guy.

When my father, Isaac, was going blind and dying, he wanted to give my twin brother, Esau, all his riches and put him in charge of everything. Esau was older than me by a little bit, so the blessing of the firstborn belonged to him. But my mother and I plotted to steal his blessing. When Isaac asked Esau to go hunting and make Isaac his favorite meal, I snuck into my father's tent while my brother was gone.

"Your voice sounds strange. Are you sure you're Esau?" Isaac asked.

"Yes, Father," I lied.

"Let me touch your arms," he said, because Esau had hairy arms. I had put goatskins over my arms to fool my dad. "Your arms are hairy like Esau's," Isaac said.

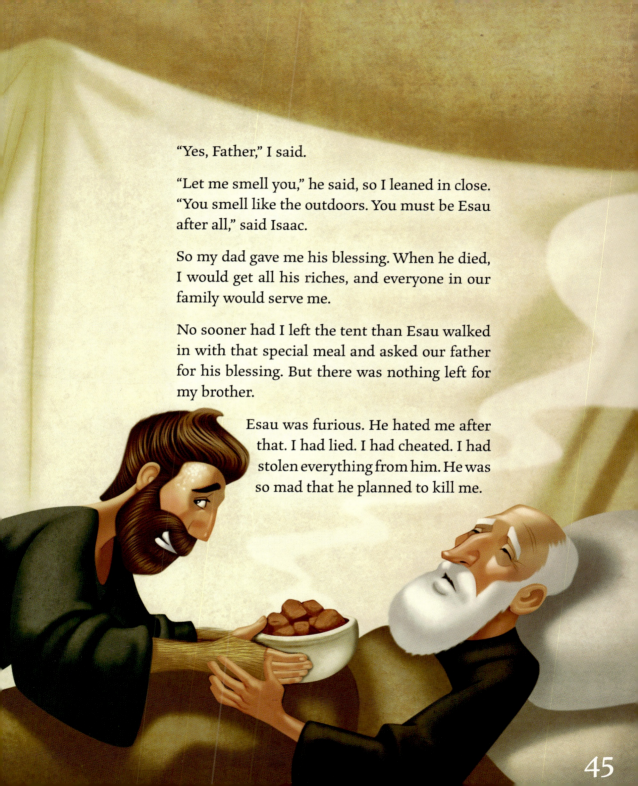

"Yes, Father," I said.

"Let me smell you," he said, so I leaned in close. "You smell like the outdoors. You must be Esau after all," said Isaac.

So my dad gave me his blessing. When he died, I would get all his riches, and everyone in our family would serve me.

No sooner had I left the tent than Esau walked in with that special meal and asked our father for his blessing. But there was nothing left for my brother.

Esau was furious. He hated me after that. I had lied. I had cheated. I had stolen everything from him. He was so mad that he planned to kill me.

45

MY mother sent me away to live with my uncle. I was gone a long time. I got married, had a family, and I owned a lot of animals. But I never forgot my brother. I wanted to make things right.

I decided to do the right thing, even if it meant Esau getting his revenge. I sent a huge gift to my brother—dozens of goats, sheep, donkeys, cows, and camels. I hoped my gift might make him a little friendlier. Turns out I didn't need to do that.

When Esau arrived, he had an army of four hundred men with him. I thought I was doomed. But when Esau saw me, he ran to me and hugged me. He forgave me, right then and there.

I didn't deserve it, but he loved me anyway. And the two of us couldn't have been happier!

47

Lying and cheating can make us feel terrible. Downright icky. Nobody likes feeling that way.

But being forgiven feels wonderful. It's freeing.

God forgives us, too. And even though we don't deserve it, God loves us. God sweeps us back into his arms every time.

Think about a time *you* did something that hurt someone else. How did that make you feel? Did you ask for forgiveness? If you need to ask someone to forgive you for something, do it today.

◟ JACOB ◞

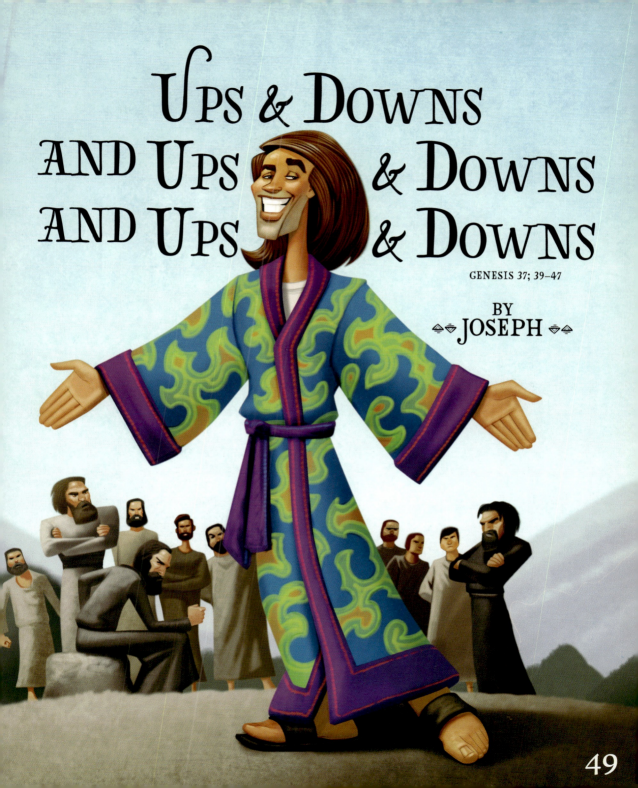

Ups & Downs and Ups & Downs and Ups & Downs

GENESIS 37; 39–47

BY ◈⬦ JOSEPH ⬦◈

IT all started with a robe.

A very nice robe, if I say so myself. It had all the colors of the rainbow. My father gave it to me because, well, I was his favorite. I may have strutted around in it a bit, too, thinking I was a prince or something. I did have dreams about people bowing to me, after all.

So it's not surprising that it really, really bugged my ten older half brothers. It bugged them so much that they began to hate me. And it wasn't long before they started planning to kill me.

And they almost did! One day they grabbed me, ripped off my robe, and sold me as a slave to some traders. Then they took my ripped-up robe, wiped some blood on it, and told our father I'd been killed by a wild animal.

That was a low point, for sure. But God was shaping my story.

51

THE traders took me to Egypt and sold me to one of Pharaoh's officers. His name was Potiphar, and I worked very hard for him. Before I knew it, he put me in charge of everything he owned. All in all, life was pretty good.

That is, until Potiphar's wife accused me of a crime I didn't commit. Potiphar was furious and threw me into prison.

Once again, I was miserable. But God was still shaping my story.

It wasn't long before the prison warden put me in charge of all the other prisoners and everything that happened in the prison. The warden trusted me; God made sure of that.

One day a couple of the other prisoners told me about some dreams they were having. Thankfully, God helped me explain them, and sure enough, their dreams came true just as I had predicted.

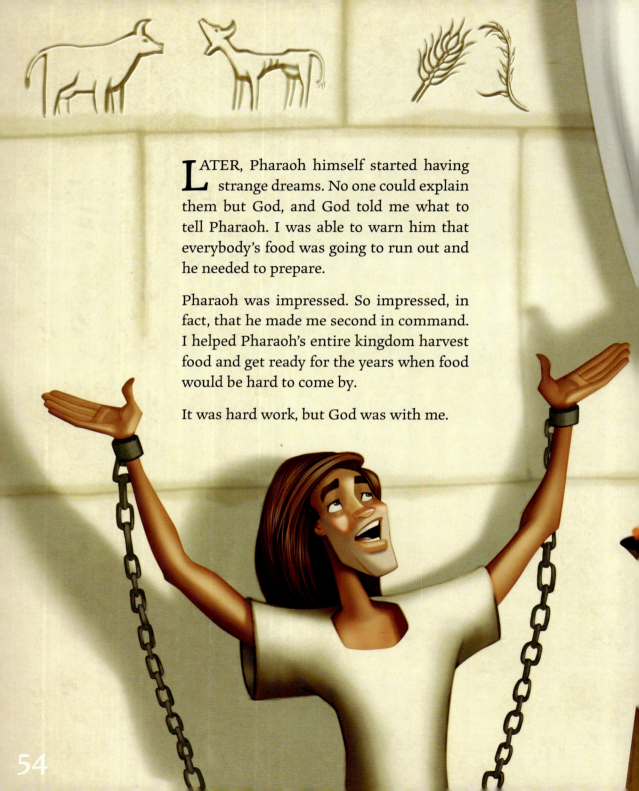

LATER, Pharaoh himself started having strange dreams. No one could explain them but God, and God told me what to tell Pharaoh. I was able to warn him that everybody's food was going to run out and he needed to prepare.

Pharaoh was impressed. So impressed, in fact, that he made me second in command. I helped Pharaoh's entire kingdom harvest food and get ready for the years when food would be hard to come by.

It was hard work, but God was with me.

54

55

WHICH brings me back to my brothers. When the famine came, people from all over came to Egypt to buy food. My brothers came, too.

When they arrived, they didn't recognize me. They even bowed to me. But I remembered them, and I remembered the old dreams I'd had as a child.

Seeing my brothers made me cry. Actually, I bawled like a baby. But I didn't let them see.

I could tell my brothers were afraid. If I had wanted, I could have had them all killed. But I loved my brothers. In a way, this wasn't really their fault. God had allowed everything to happen—all the ups and downs in my life—so that I could SAVE their lives.

My story has a happy ending. My father and all my brothers and their families moved close to me in Egypt. They had everything they needed and lived long and happy lives.

God was with me, and God was with my family.

I never had any doubt that God was with me. Every step of the way, through the good and the bad (as well as the very good and very bad), God was there.

It's amazing to think that God worked everything out for good in my life so that I could help my family. If I hadn't been sold as a slave by my brothers, I wouldn't have been able to give them food during the hungry years.

What kinds of difficult things have *you* had to go through? Hard times at school? Sad times with your friends? Find a piece of colored paper and write "God is with me!" on it. Then put it in a place where you'll see it every day.

✕ JOSEPH ✕

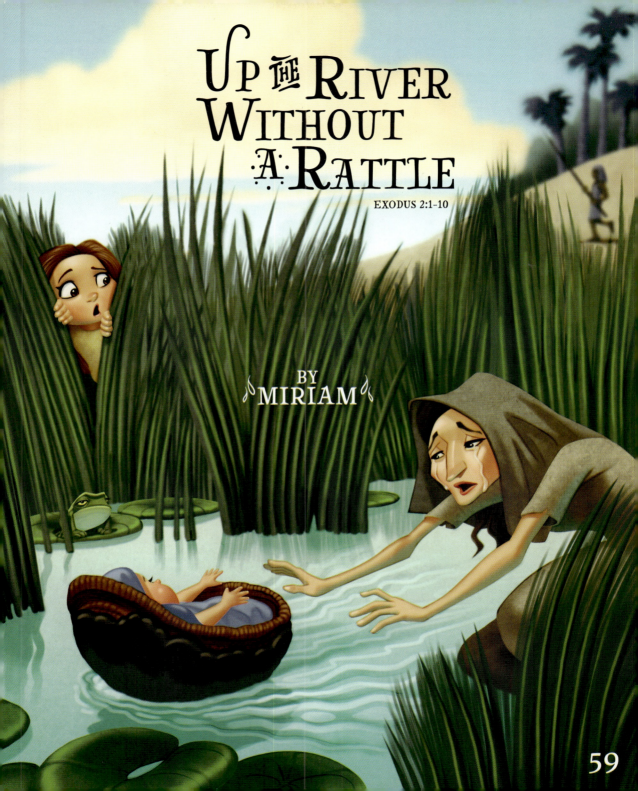

Up the River Without a Rattle

EXODUS 2:1-10

BY MIRIAM

MY baby brother is so cute!

Seriously, he's adorable. And he's special, too. My mother said so. She told me there's something about him—that God has big plans for him some day.

But he's in danger—big danger! There's a new Pharaoh here in Egypt, and he doesn't like us Hebrews. He wants to kill all of our baby boys!

My mom knew if any Egyptians saw my little brother, they would end his life. So with tears in her eyes, she laid him in a basket and put him in the Nile River. She hoped that somehow God would keep him safe.

I just couldn't stand to watch him go. So I hid in the reeds on the bank of the river and kept a close eye on that basket. I knew God was watching, too.

It wasn't long before the Egyptian princess herself—Pharaoh's daughter—came down to take a bath in the river. She saw the basket right away and told her servants to fetch it for her.

I held my breath and watched.

THE baby was crying as the princess pulled him out of the basket. But instead of throwing him in the river, she hugged him and held him close. I could see in her eyes that she felt sorry for him.

I saw my chance. I ran up to the princess and said, "Would you like me to find a Hebrew woman to nurse the baby for you?"

"Yes, please!" the princess said.

So I ran back home as fast as I could and told my mother. The princess asked her to feed and take care of my brother till he was a little older. She even paid us!

My baby brother is special, all right. Not only did God save his life, but he also got to grow up in Pharaoh's palace. God had an incredible plan in store for my brother. The princess even gave him a special name.

She called him Moses.

God takes care of the people he loves. I know that for a fact. I watched it happen with my own eyes. Just when it seemed certain my baby brother would be killed, God saved him.

Moses may have been my little brother, but he was God's child, too. And you know what? YOU are God's child, too! God loves you and has special plans for your life, just like he did for Moses and me.

What do *you* think God has in store for your life? What's one special thing you can do? Do that special thing today!

⇐ MIRIAM ⇒

The GREAT ESCAPE

EXODUS 12:1-42;
14:5-31

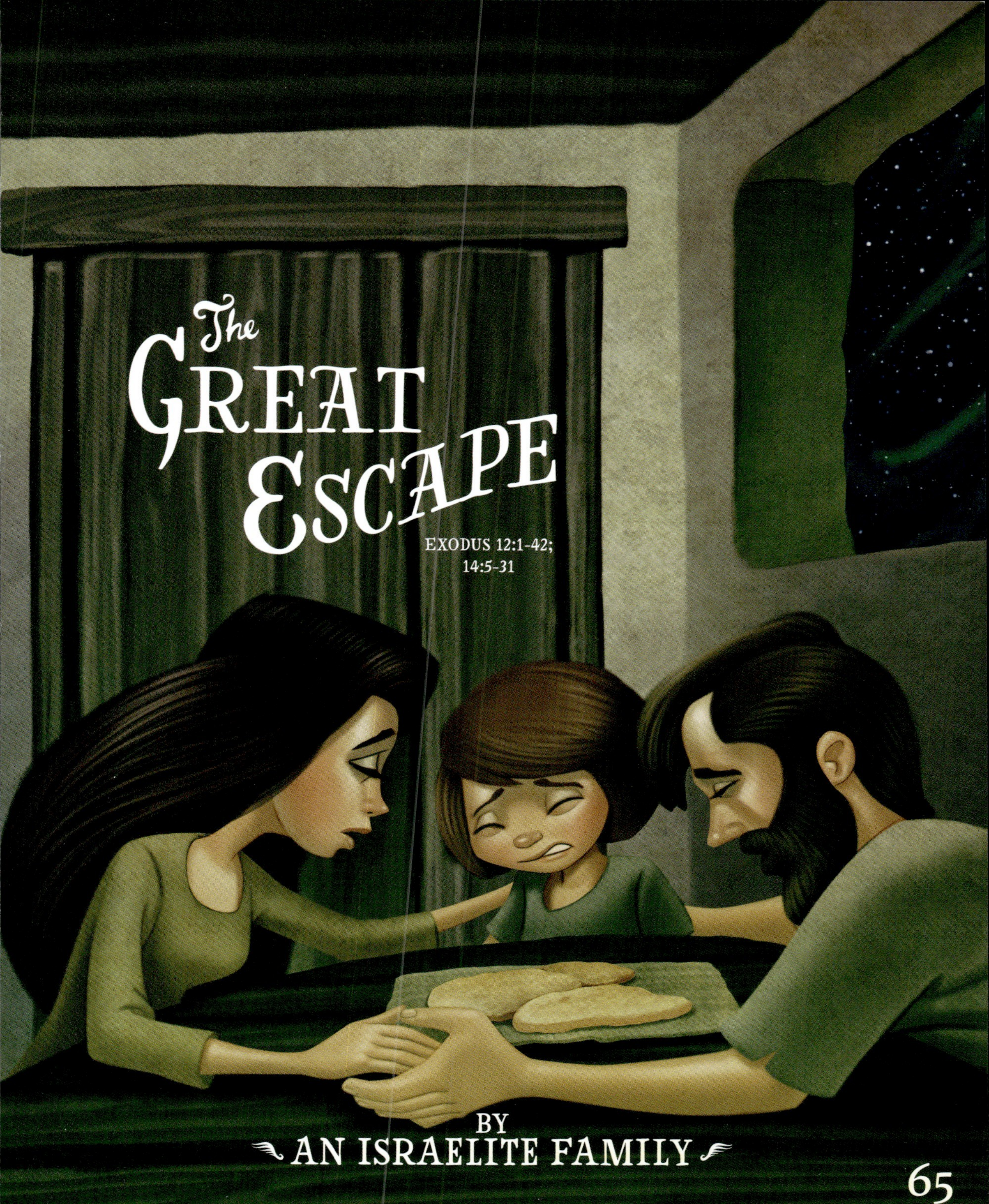

BY
~ AN ISRAELITE FAMILY ~

65

THESE were dark times.

God had just sent nine terrible plagues over Egypt—gnats, flies, frogs, hail—you name it. But Pharaoh still wouldn't let God's people—the Israelites—go. And now the tenth and final plague was upon us: Death was coming.

But even in this blackest of nights, we had hope. God promised to rescue us, although the firstborn sons of Egypt would die.

God said he would "pass over" the houses of his people who put the blood of a lamb over their front doors. While we huddled with our families over our Passover meals, I was scared. After all, I was the firstborn son in my family.

Safe in my home, I heard the screams and cries of Egyptian parents as their firstborn sons died. The tenth plague was both quick and merciless.

Before the night was over, Pharaoh called Moses and Aaron, who was Moses' older brother, to his palace. Pharaoh's own son had died, too. With tears streaming down his angry face, he pointed toward the hills and yelled, "Get out!"

And just like that, all of us Israelites—more than a million of us—quickly packed up our things and hurried out of Egypt.

But we weren't safe yet.

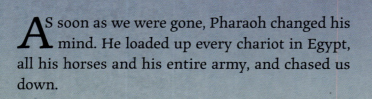

AS soon as we were gone, Pharaoh changed his mind. He loaded up every chariot in Egypt, all his horses and his entire army, and chased us down.

By the time we saw them coming, there was no way for us to escape. We were backed up against the sea with nowhere to run. Of course, we panicked.

"Oh no!" we shouted. "We're doomed! We've escaped Egypt, only to die in the wilderness!"

"Stay calm," Moses said. "Just stand still and watch God rescue you."

As usual, Moses was right. God took care of us... again. God's angel went to the back of our camp to protect us. Then the huge pillar of cloud that had been leading us moved behind to block the Egyptians' path. It hovered there all day, and at night it turned into fire.

And then God did something even more amazing.

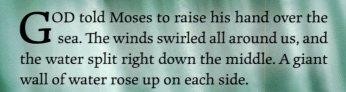

GOD told Moses to raise his hand over the sea. The winds swirled all around us, and the water split right down the middle. A giant wall of water rose up on each side.

God created a dry path for us to cross the sea!

We picked up our things and began to walk across the seabed, with walls of water on each side! Not a drop of water splashed our faces or touched our feet.

Meanwhile, Pharaoh watched in amazement. His anger turned into rage, and he shouted for his army to follow us. When we glanced back over our shoulders, we could see the soldiers racing their chariots into the seabed behind us.

They were catching up, and fast.

BUT we kept moving. God was doing something miraculous, and all we could do was push onward.

When every one of us reached the other side of the sea, God told Moses to raise his hand again. The walls of water rushed down over the dry path, filling the sea with water again.

Wave after wave crashed down on Pharaoh's soldiers and chariots. Next thing we knew, the entire army had been covered in water; not one of them survived. They were gone.

We stood in awe of God's mighty power. We laughed and cried and hugged each other. More than four hundred years of slavery in Egypt had finally come to an end.

God had truly rescued us.

And we were finally free!

We're a family. We love each other and grow closer to each other every day.

We've gone through some scary times together, from living through that awful night in Egypt to escaping through those giant walls of water. But we stuck together and trusted God.

YOU are a part of a family, too. And sometimes you go through times that are kind of scary or make you nervous. But God wants you and your family to stick together. As long as you trust God, you can make it!

What does it feel like to be afraid? Imagine yourself in a scary situation. Now think of yourself being completely safe. How different does it feel to have no fear?

AN ISRAELITE FAMILY

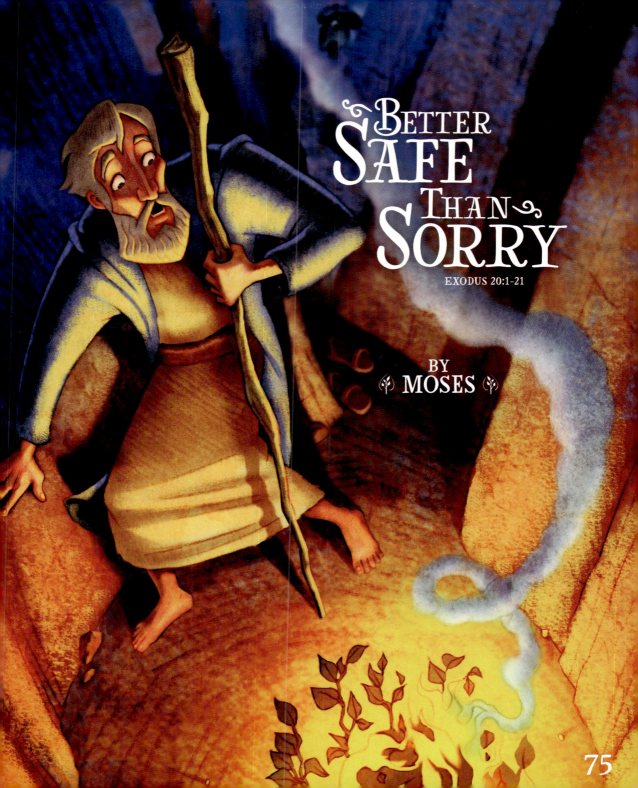

BETTER SAFE THAN SORRY

EXODUS 20:1-21

BY ❧ MOSES ❧

NO doubt about it, I've lived through some incredible adventures. From the time I was born, I've faced things in my life that no one else in all of history has experienced.

Every step of the way, through every breath and every day, God has been there with me.

God was with me when Pharaoh's daughter plucked me out of the river to save my life.

God spoke to me through a burning bush. God was there when I raised my hand and parted the Red Sea. God gave our army one victory after another in battle. And God even provided food from heaven when my people were hungry.

God always took care of me.

77

GOD had another special way of taking care of his people. After God rescued us from the Egyptians, he sent me up to the top of Mount Sinai. He gave me ten instructions to help us live good lives that please him and keep us from hurting God and each other. These instructions are called the Ten Commandments, and this is what they say:

1. I am your God, and your only God.

2. Do not make any false gods and worship them.

3. Do not misuse God's name.

4. Rest on the Sabbath, and keep the day holy.

5. Honor your parents.

6. Do not murder.

7. Stay true to you husband or wife.

8. Do not steal.

9. Do not lie.

10. Do not want what others have.

If God's people can follow these simple instructions, they'll live happier lives that please God.

When you love something, you want to take care of it. I worked hard in my life to protect and help God's people. I did it because I loved them.

God loves you, too. And God wants what's best for you. God has written down instructions in the Bible to keep us close to him. When we follow those instructions, we'll live good lives that please God, and we won't hurt our family and friends—or our very best friend, God.

Lying is one of the rules a lot of people break. Think about a time *you* didn't tell the truth to someone who cares about you. How do you think it made that person feel to be lied to? Pray to God and ask him to help you always tell the truth.

MOSES

Following the Crowd

EXODUS 32:1-29

BY AARON

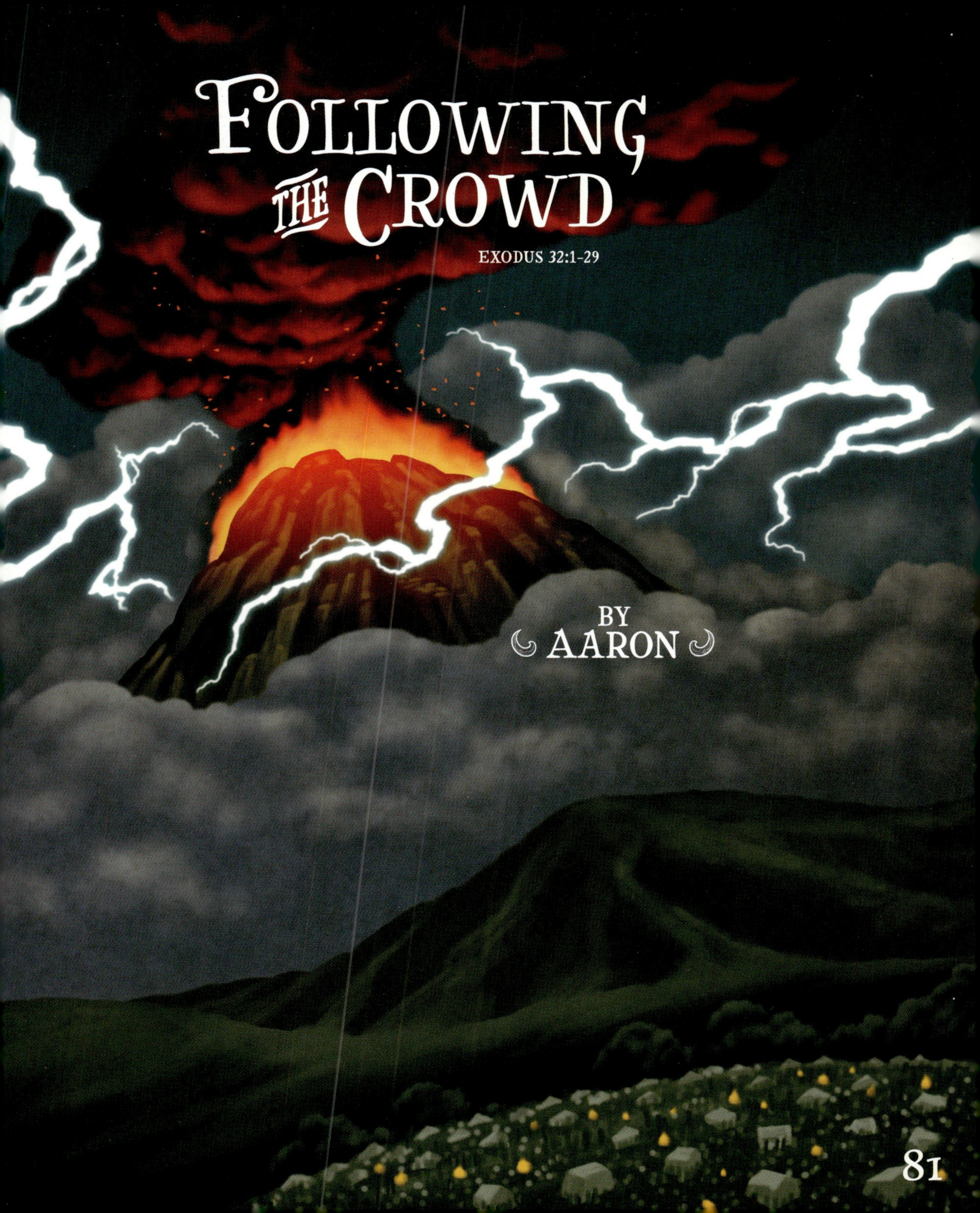

LOOK, it wasn't my fault. Not really.

I mean, the people were getting really impatient. Moses had been up on that mountain for who knows how long. For all they knew, he was long gone. And they wanted some new gods to worship.

What else could I do?

I only did what they wanted me to do. I had them put all their gold in a big pile, and we melted it down. Then we shaped it into a giant gold calf. And let me tell you, they loved it!

The next morning they started bowing down to it and giving it offerings. They were singing and dancing and eating and drinking. There's nothing wrong with a little party, is there? Honestly, I'd never seen them so happy!

But then God told Moses to go back down the mountain. And when he returned to us, Moses was not happy. Not one bit.

I'D never seen Moses so angry.

The first thing Moses did was smash the tablets with the Ten Commandments to the ground. Then he melted the golden calf, ground it into dust, threw it into the water, and made everyone drink it.

(It did *not* taste good.)

Then Moses let me have it. "How could you let this happen?"

I did the first thing that popped into my head: I blamed everyone else.

"It's not my fault! These people are evil. They made me do it!" I cried, pointing my finger at all the people behind me.

Needless to say, we were in trouble—big time. God was not pleased. And now I felt terrible because I really let God—and Moses—down.

Okay, okay, okay. I get it now.

I didn't stand up for what I knew was right. I caved in. I followed the crowd. Then I pointed fingers.

I was a coward.

It wasn't my brightest moment, that's for sure.

That's why I'm so thankful that God can forgive me. Even through my worst behavior, God still loves me. God still has a plan for my future. God can still use me to do good.

Be honest: Has there ever been a time you should've stood up for what's right? Sometimes it can be hard going against the crowd. But let me assure you, standing up for the right thing is *always* the right thing.

◢AARON◣

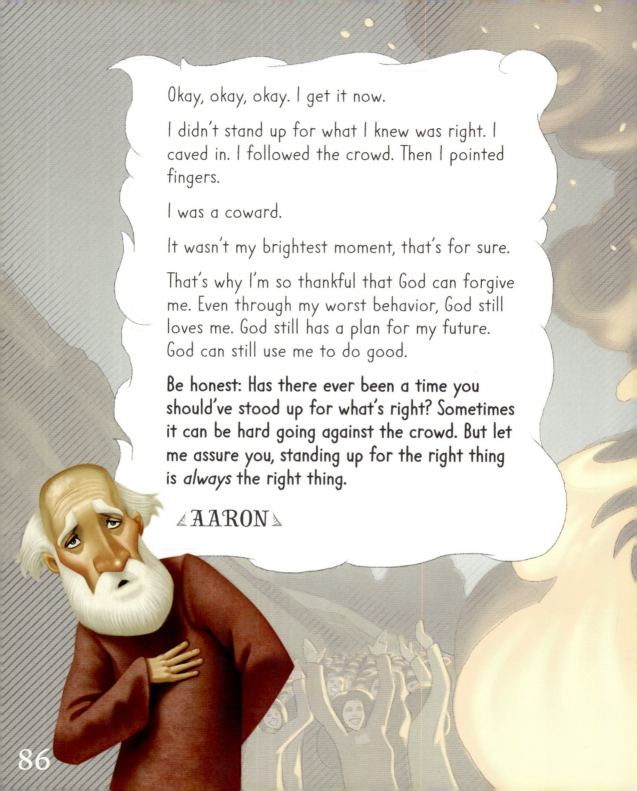

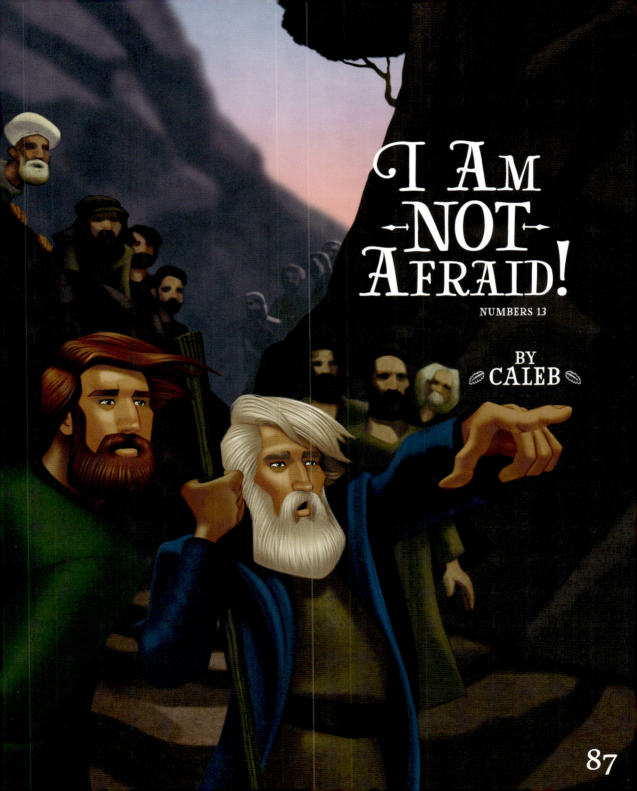

I Am Not Afraid!

NUMBERS 13

BY ~ CALEB ~

A long time ago, God promised to give us, his people, a very special place to call home. We call it the Promised Land. And we're almost there!

The problem is, we can't just walk in and unpack. Some of our enemies are already living there. So our leader, Moses, told twelve of us to sneak into the country and spy on it.

As we climbed over the hills and snuck through the land, we were amazed at what we saw. The soil was rich. The rivers sparkled. Fruit trees grew everywhere with more figs and pomegranates than I've ever seen. The clusters of grapes were so huge it took two of us to carry them!

It was a land flowing with milk and honey. I couldn't *wait* to pack my bags and move in!

The other spies weren't so sure, though.

WHEN we returned to Moses to report what we had seen, we showed him the bounty of fruit we had found. Joshua and I were excited, but the ten other spies were afraid and had different ideas.

"Sure, there's more food than we could ever have imagined," they said. "But the people living there are GIANTS. Their walls are big. And they're so strong! Those giants would smash us like little grasshoppers!"

I couldn't believe what I was hearing. God had promised us this land. It was ours for the taking!

"I say we go right now. We'll conquer it for sure!" I said. "All we need to do is trust God and have some courage."

91

People say I'm courageous. I guess they're right; I wasn't afraid of marching into the Promised Land and making it our home. But I don't think it's hard to find courage when you know God is on your side.

After all, when God promises you something, what's there to be afraid of? God is way bigger than our fears.

And guess what? Later we did make it our home! Thanks to God, and God alone.

What are *you* afraid of in your life? Did you know God is on your side? Think of one area where you need some courage. Then pray and ask God to give you all the courage you need.

꧁CALEB꧂

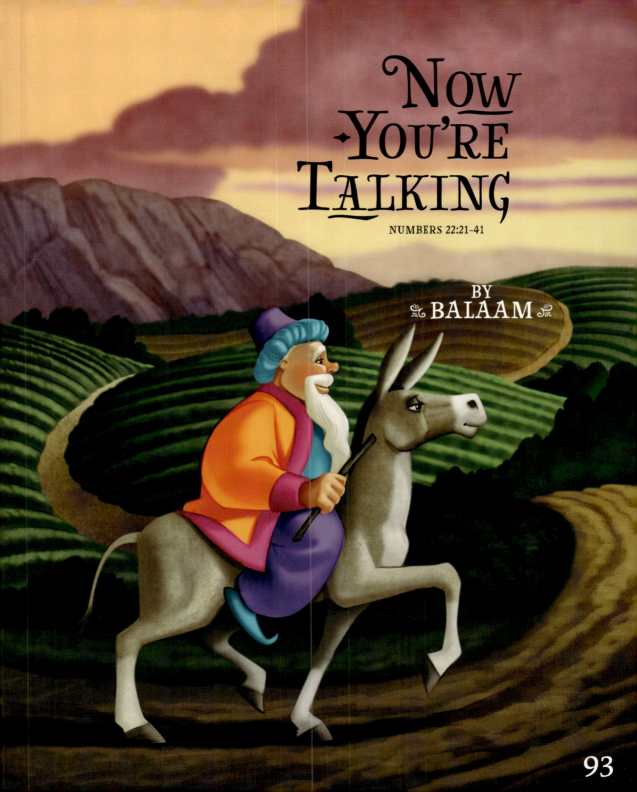

Now You're Talking

NUMBERS 22:21-41

BY ❧ BALAAM ❧

I love my donkey. We've been together for years. Sure, he can be stubborn sometimes; all donkeys are like that. But today he was especially headstrong.

I had been traveling down the road to visit the king of Moab. But God wanted to stop me from going, so God sent an angel with a drawn sword to block my path.

I didn't see the angel. But my donkey did, and he bolted off the road into the weeds. I hit him with my stick and got him back on the road.

The angel appeared again, but I still didn't see it. This time my donkey tried to squeeze around the angel and crushed my foot against the wall. So I hit him again.

Then the angel showed up one more time, and my donkey dropped to the ground...with me still on his back! I was so mad! This time I let my donkey have it.

THEN I got the surprise of my life: My donkey started talking to me!

"Why do you keep hitting me?" my donkey asked.

"You're making me look like a fool!" I shouted. "You've never done anything like this before!"

"Exactly," said my donkey.

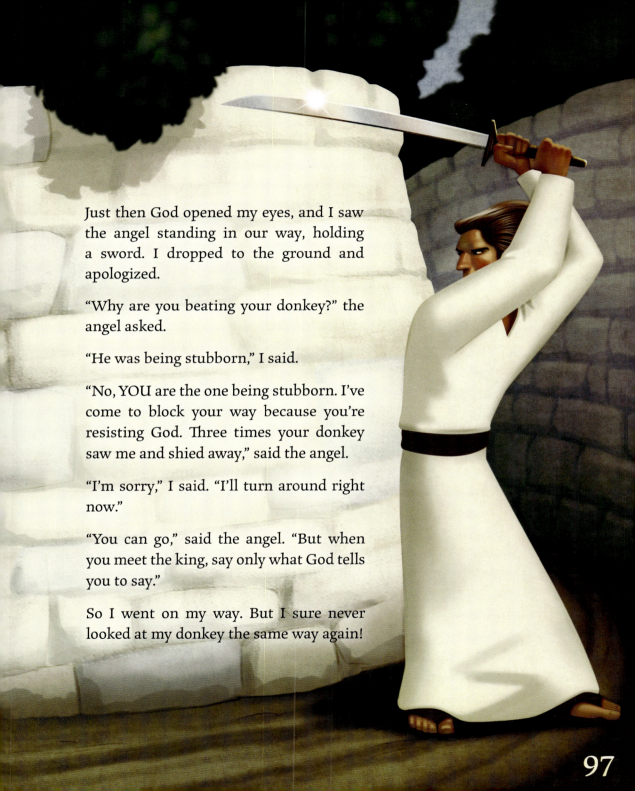

Just then God opened my eyes, and I saw the angel standing in our way, holding a sword. I dropped to the ground and apologized.

"Why are you beating your donkey?" the angel asked.

"He was being stubborn," I said.

"No, YOU are the one being stubborn. I've come to block your way because you're resisting God. Three times your donkey saw me and shied away," said the angel.

"I'm sorry," I said. "I'll turn around right now."

"You can go," said the angel. "But when you meet the king, say only what God tells you to say."

So I went on my way. But I sure never looked at my donkey the same way again!

When God wants to get your attention, sometimes it takes something extraordinary. It can be the voice of a friend—even an unexpected friend with four legs and big ears.

I only wish my donkey would talk to me again!

Don't get me wrong; I've always tried to be faithful to God. People who know me know that I try to do what God wants me to do.

But sometimes I get a little off track. Does that ever happen to you? Then God has a way of surprising us sometimes. A little extra push or a nudge, maybe even a jolt. Anything to get our feet back on God's path.

How has God tried to get *your* attention? Find a piece of paper and write down five things that distract you from God. Then pray and ask God to help you remember to focus on him instead.

BALAAM

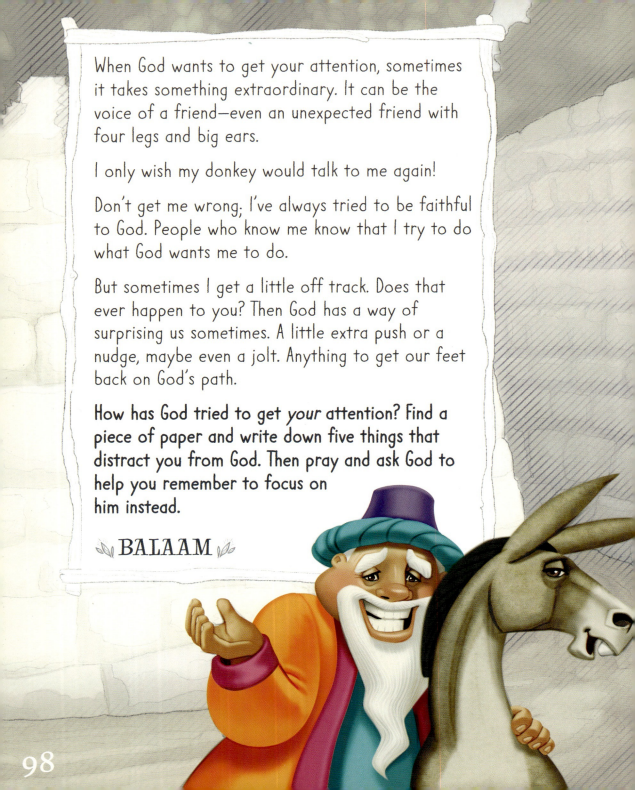

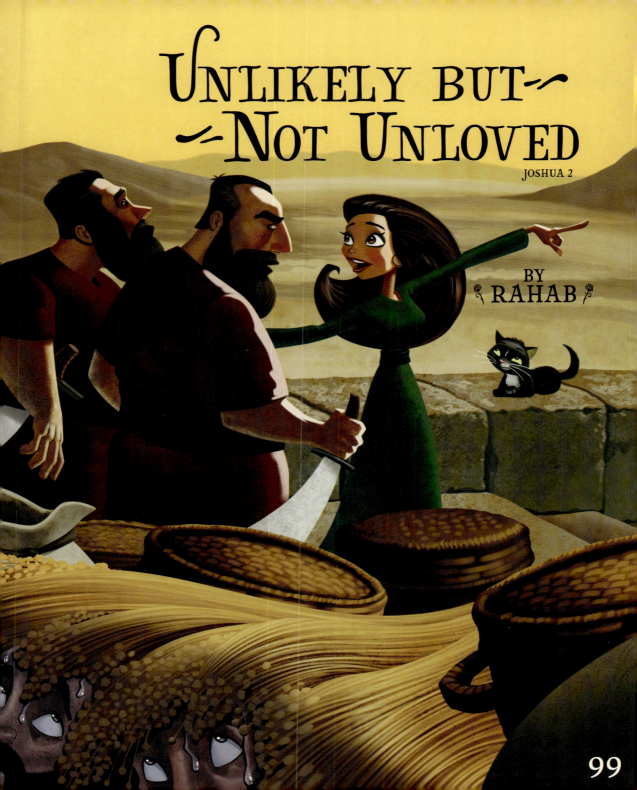

Unlikely but ~ ~ Not Unloved

JOSHUA 2

BY ~ RAHAB ~

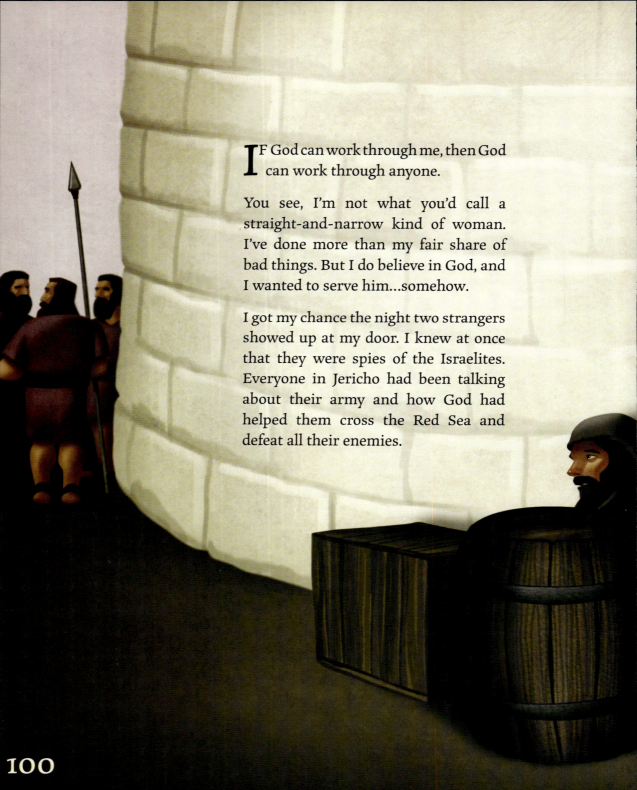

IF God can work through me, then God can work through anyone.

You see, I'm not what you'd call a straight-and-narrow kind of woman. I've done more than my fair share of bad things. But I do believe in God, and I wanted to serve him...somehow.

I got my chance the night two strangers showed up at my door. I knew at once that they were spies of the Israelites. Everyone in Jericho had been talking about their army and how God had helped them cross the Red Sea and defeat all their enemies.

We were terrified of them!

But I knew God loved them, so I decided to help them. I let them hide on my roof while the Jericho guards stopped by to search for them. I even lied to keep them safe.

I knew their people would return soon to destroy Jericho, and I had one request.

"Since I helped you, will you spare my family?" I asked.

"Yes," the spies told me. "Just hang this red rope out your window. When our army overtakes Jericho, your family will be safe—as long as they're in your house."

I agreed. I helped them climb out the window and made sure they got away without a scratch. And I left that red rope outside my window until the Israelite army came back.

Now I'll live the rest of my life worshipping the one true God, the God who loves me!

I'm living proof that God doesn't work only through the strongest, or the wisest, or the most famous. When I think about all the bad things I've done, I'm probably the least likely person God would want in his family.

Yet God chose *me*. God let me be a key part of his grand plan. I'll always be grateful for that.

God has chosen you, too. God loves you, and he wants to work through you to love other people. It doesn't matter who you are. Your gifts and talents can be a blessing to others.

God made *you* special. Maybe you're a good listener or you give big hugs. How can you use your special talents to serve God?

⊱ RAHAB ⊰

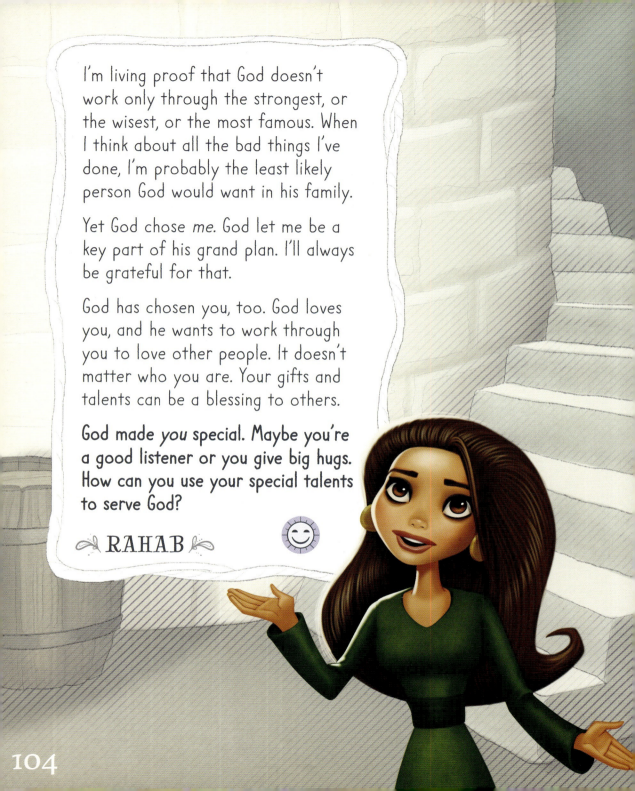

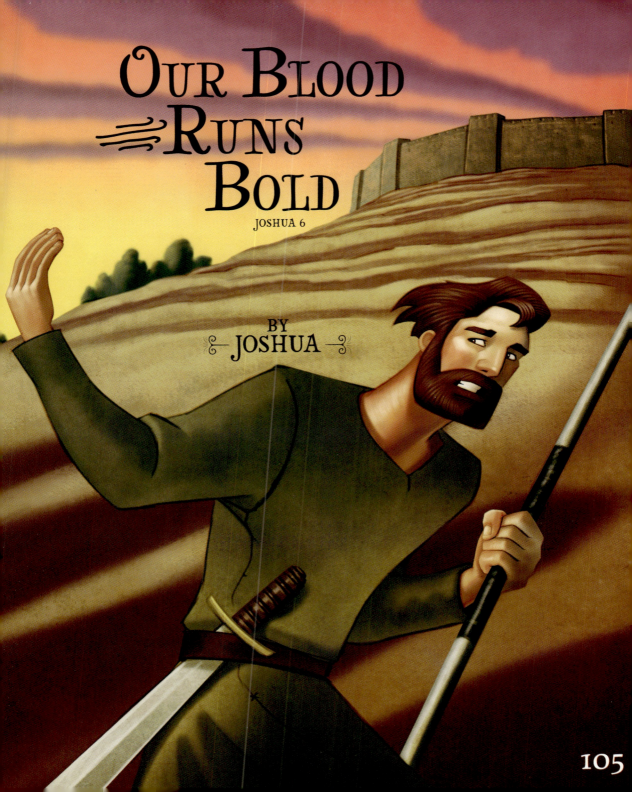

Our Blood Runs Bold

JOSHUA 6

BY ❧ JOSHUA ☙

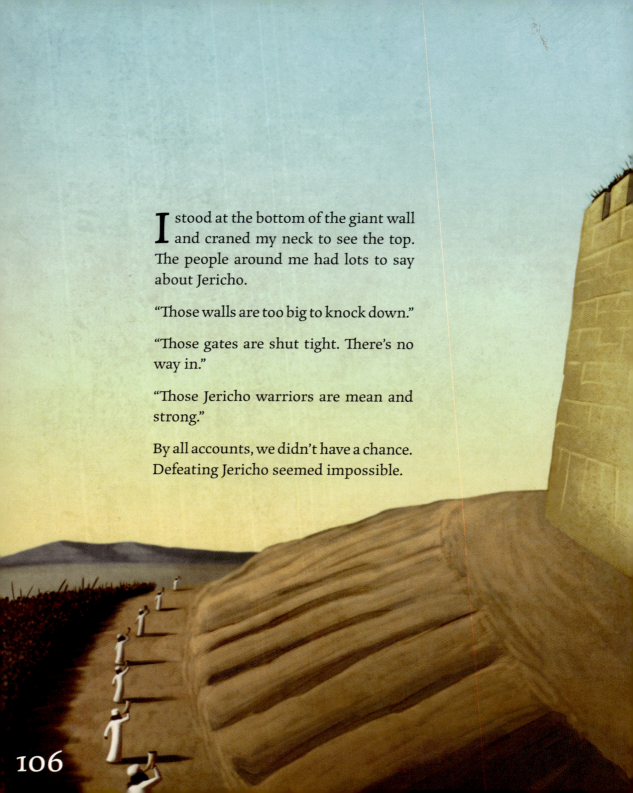

I stood at the bottom of the giant wall and craned my neck to see the top. The people around me had lots to say about Jericho.

"Those walls are too big to knock down."

"Those gates are shut tight. There's no way in."

"Those Jericho warriors are mean and strong."

By all accounts, we didn't have a chance. Defeating Jericho seemed impossible.

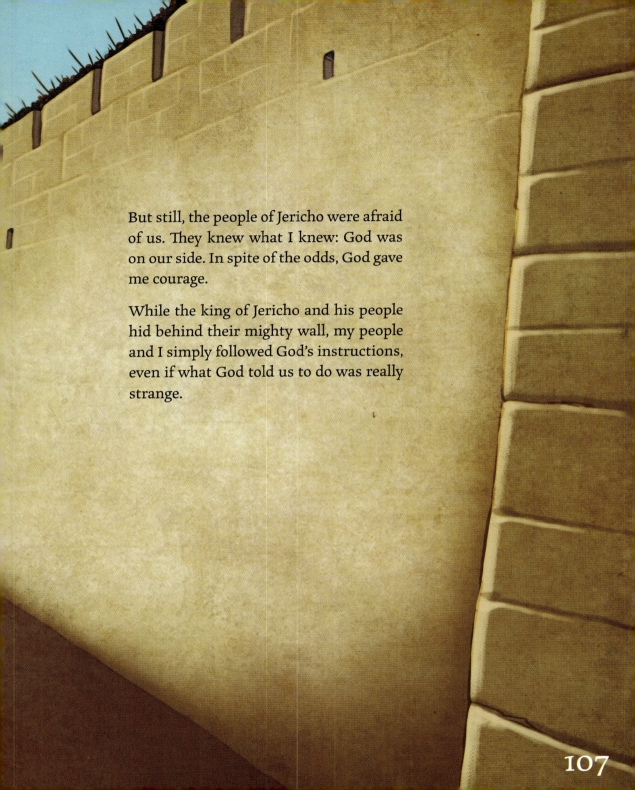

But still, the people of Jericho were afraid of us. They knew what I knew: God was on our side. In spite of the odds, God gave me courage.

While the king of Jericho and his people hid behind their mighty wall, my people and I simply followed God's instructions, even if what God told us to do was really strange.

WE silently marched around the town once a day for six days. On the seventh day, everyone marched around the town seven times. When we stopped, our priests blew their horns as loud as they could. And then everyone shouted as loud as they could.

The great walls of Jericho shook, cracked, and thundered to the ground. Our enemy was defeated.

We didn't win the battle with stronger men or sharper swords. We won with courage: God-given courage.

As promised, God spared Rahab and her family. And she lives with us to this day! But as for the rest of Jericho, it was nothing but a pile of rubble.

Courage isn't an easy thing. Sometimes it doesn't even make sense. But it's a MUST whenever you're facing a situation that seems impossible.

There was no logical way for us to defeat Jericho. We didn't fight with hammers or battering rams or swords. We went to battle with one thing: courage.

Of course, our courage came from God.

In the end it was our voices that caused the walls to crash down. God has given each of us a voice; a voice to tell others about God's love and a voice to speak words that lift up and honor God.

In what way can *you* use your voice to bring a message of God's love to the world around you? Do you have the courage to tell others about God? I promise you, God will be with you just as he was with me.

◣JOSHUA◢

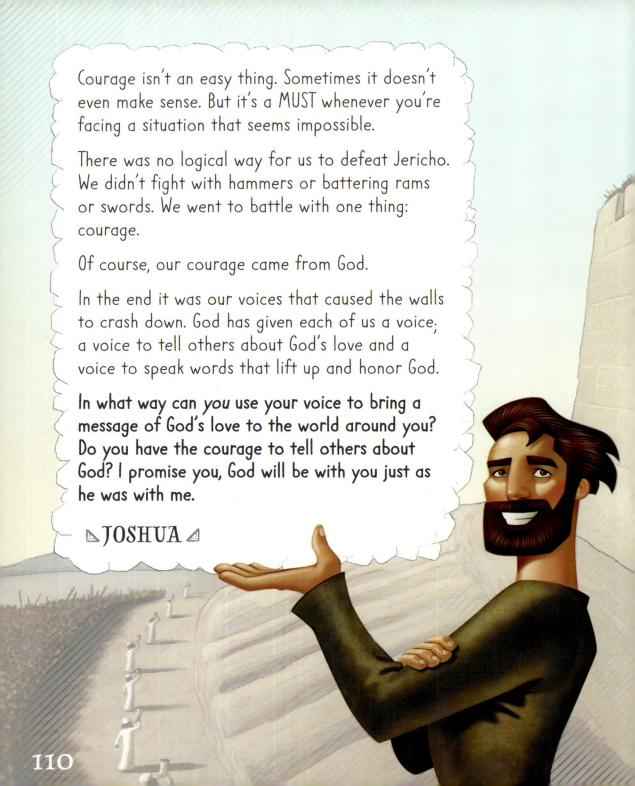

I hate to say it, but we Israelites change our minds a lot.

One day we're worshipping God and giving thanks, and the next day we're back to our old wicked ways. We just can't seem to stay out of trouble.

I was a leader for Israel during a time like this. For twenty years we'd been under the control of King Jabin, and he treated us like rats. The people of Israel begged God to save them.

God told me to have a man named Barak gather ten thousand soldiers to fight the nasty king's army, led by Commander Sisera. But Barak wouldn't do it unless I went with him. So I went, of course, because it's always wise to follow God's instructions.

I told them to fight, and fight they did. Long story short, we won—big time.

113

SOMEHOW Commander Sisera escaped. While all of his soldiers were being killed, he ran off to hide.

But Sisera made a BIG mistake. He ran into a woman named Jael. She offered Sisera some milk and let him hide in her tent. But while Sisera was fast asleep, Jael took care of that evil man. Let's just say he never drank milk again.

Our army got stronger and stronger after that. We finally defeated King Jabin, and God gave us our freedom once again.

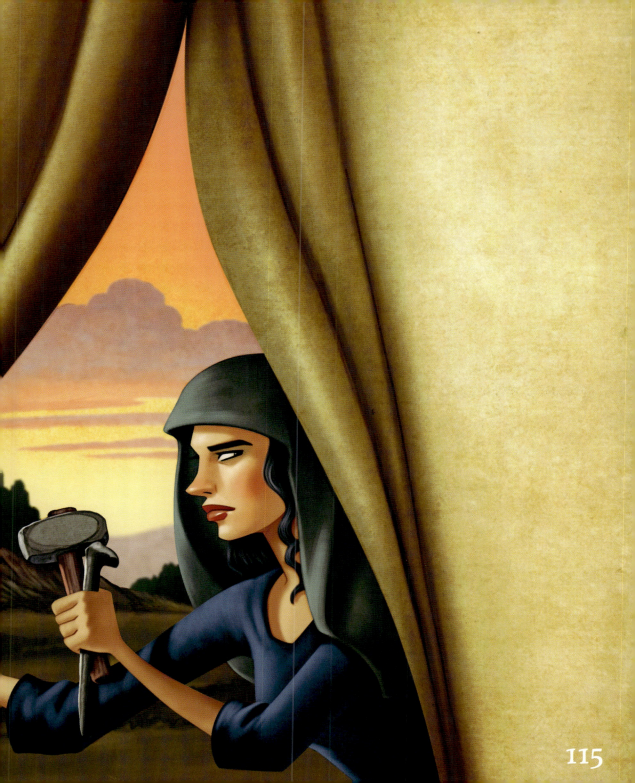

I have to be honest. It hasn't been easy being a woman during these difficult times. Women don't get many chances to be leaders in this world of ours. So when the chance comes, it's important to stay close to God.

It's also not easy being wise, especially when everyone around you is acting foolish. That's why I depend on God. God gives me wisdom and helps me make the right choices.

Every man, woman, and child can get wisdom from God. That includes you. And all you have to do is ask him for it!

Could *you* use some wisdom in your life right now? Are you trying to decide what's the best thing to do? Pray and ask God right now to give you wisdom. He will!

➤➤ DEBORAH ◄

Who, Me?

JUDGES 6–7

BY
GIDEON

THE Midianites were awful, cruel, terrible people. They wrecked all our crops, stole our animals, and left us nothing to eat.

Someone had to do something.

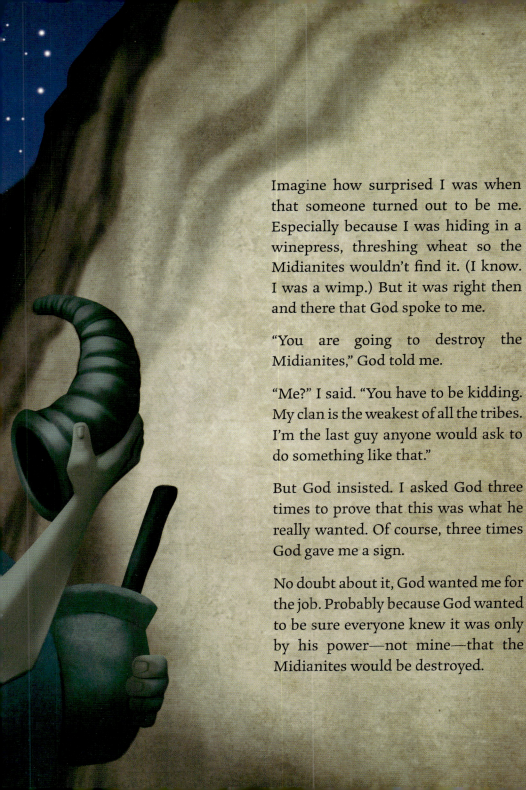

Imagine how surprised I was when that someone turned out to be me. Especially because I was hiding in a winepress, threshing wheat so the Midianites wouldn't find it. (I know. I was a wimp.) But it was right then and there that God spoke to me.

"You are going to destroy the Midianites," God told me.

"Me?" I said. "You have to be kidding. My clan is the weakest of all the tribes. I'm the last guy anyone would ask to do something like that."

But God insisted. I asked God three times to prove that this was what he really wanted. Of course, three times God gave me a sign.

No doubt about it, God wanted me for the job. Probably because God wanted to be sure everyone knew it was only by his power—not mine—that the Midianites would be destroyed.

THEIR army was so gigantic that there were too many soldiers to count. So I needed to form the biggest army I could muster.

But God had other plans.

I started by gathering thirty-two thousand men. God said that was too many. If we won we could say it was because of *our* strength, not God's. So I sent home all who were afraid to fight. That left me with ten thousand soldiers. But that was still far more than God wanted.

After one more test, three hundred men were left.

Three hundred versus too many to count. I hoped God knew what he was doing.

We waited till it was dark. I gave each man a ram's horn and a torch inside a clay jar. We scattered around the hills surrounding the massive army below. Then, at the same time, we blew our horns, cracked open our torches, and shouted, "For the Lord and for Gideon!"

The Midianites panicked. God made them so confused that they started fighting each other. We beat them without raising a single sword!

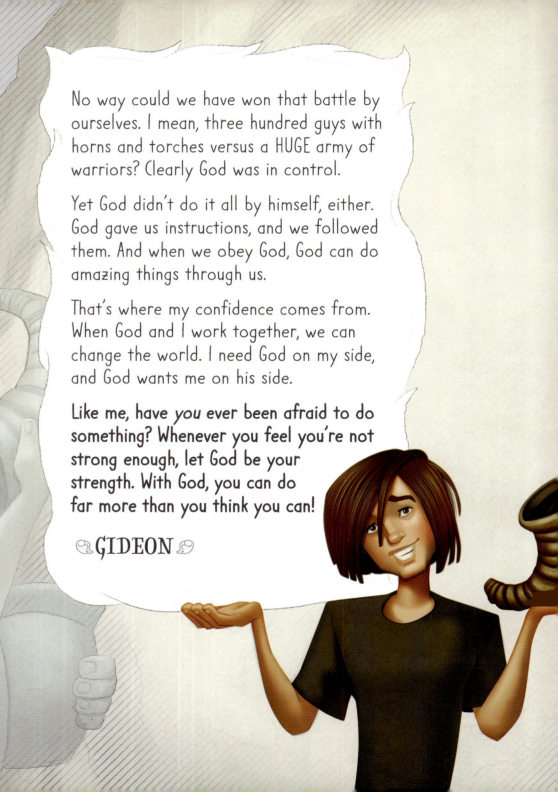

No way could we have won that battle by ourselves. I mean, three hundred guys with horns and torches versus a HUGE army of warriors? Clearly God was in control.

Yet God didn't do it all by himself, either. God gave us instructions, and we followed them. And when we obey God, God can do amazing things through us.

That's where my confidence comes from. When God and I work together, we can change the world. I need God on my side, and God wants me on his side.

Like me, have *you* ever been afraid to do something? Whenever you feel you're not strong enough, let God be your strength. With God, you can do far more than you think you can!

GIDEON

Keeping It Together

Ruth 1–2

BY RUTH and NAOMI

MY name is Naomi. If there's one thing you need to know about me, it's that I lost the most important people in my life. First my husband died, and then both of my sons died. My sons' wives, Ruth and Orpah, were the only family I had left.

I told them to go back home to their own mothers, but Ruth wouldn't budge. She told me something I'll never forget:

"Where you go, I will go. Where you live, I will live. Your people will be my people, and your God will be my God."

I was so touched. So we started our journey *together*. When we got to my hometown of Bethlehem, we were both welcomed with open arms. Ruth, faithful friend that she is, went straight to work gathering grain in the fields.

I'M Ruth, Naomi's daughter-in-law. And Naomi's right; I wanted to do my part to help us both have something to eat and live a good life.

But it wasn't easy. Farming is hard work. I went to a nearby barley field and picked up the extra grain the harvesters left behind.

Soon the owner of the field saw me working. His name was Boaz, and he'd heard about what a true friend I'd been to Naomi and how I'd left my own family to help her. He was amazed at my loyalty.

Boaz gave me food and water. He watched out for me, and he let me gather grain as long as I wanted.

I showed Naomi all the food I collected. She was so excited! I knew I had made the right choice in being Naomi's best friend.

Friendship is one of the most special gifts God has given us. Friends support each other, encourage each other, and help each other through every step of life.

The two of us are best friends. But we're not just friends with each other, we're friends with God, too.

Having a relationship with God is just like a friendship. You spend time together, talk to each other, and honor each other. God is the best friend you could *ever* hope for.

Think about one of *your* best friends. What do you like to do together? What do you like most about your friend? What's one way being friends with that person is like being friends with God?

RUTH *and* NAOMI

A Prayer and a Promise

1 Samuel 1:9-28

By Hannah

THERE was only one thing I wanted in life: a son. But year after year went by, and nothing. No child. Was it never going to happen?

I went to the Tabernacle to beg God to give me a boy. I even made a promise. If God would give me a son, I would give him back to God.

I was crying and praying out loud. I must have looked strange! Eli, the priest, asked me what was wrong. When I told him how sad I was, Eli assured me that God would answer my prayer.

And God did!

I named my beautiful baby boy Samuel. I loved him so much! I took care of him, and when he was just a few years old, I took him back to Eli at the Tabernacle.

It was such an honor to dedicate Samuel to God. He served God for the rest of his life.

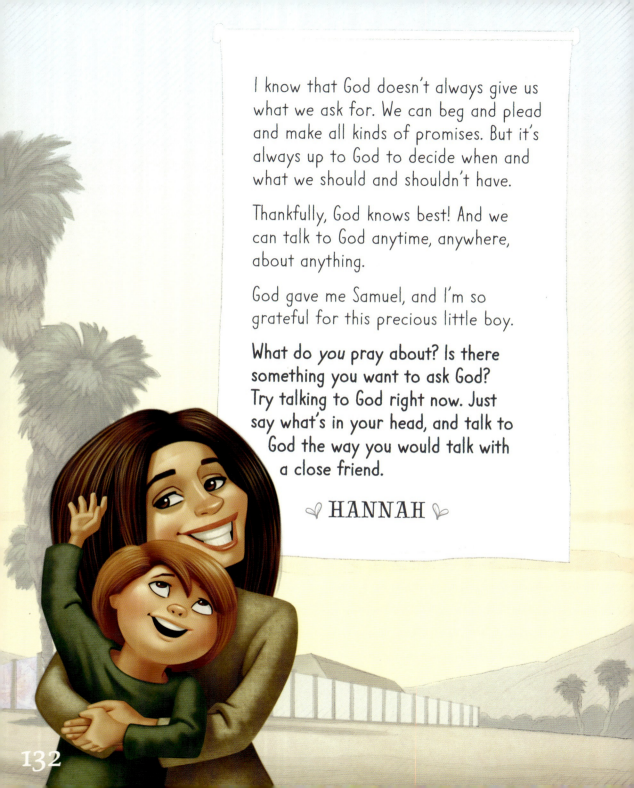

I know that God doesn't always give us what we ask for. We can beg and plead and make all kinds of promises. But it's always up to God to decide when and what we should and shouldn't have.

Thankfully, God knows best! And we can talk to God anytime, anywhere, about anything.

God gave me Samuel, and I'm so grateful for this precious little boy.

What do *you* pray about? Is there something you want to ask God? Try talking to God right now. Just say what's in your head, and talk to God the way you would talk with a close friend.

☙ HANNAH ❧

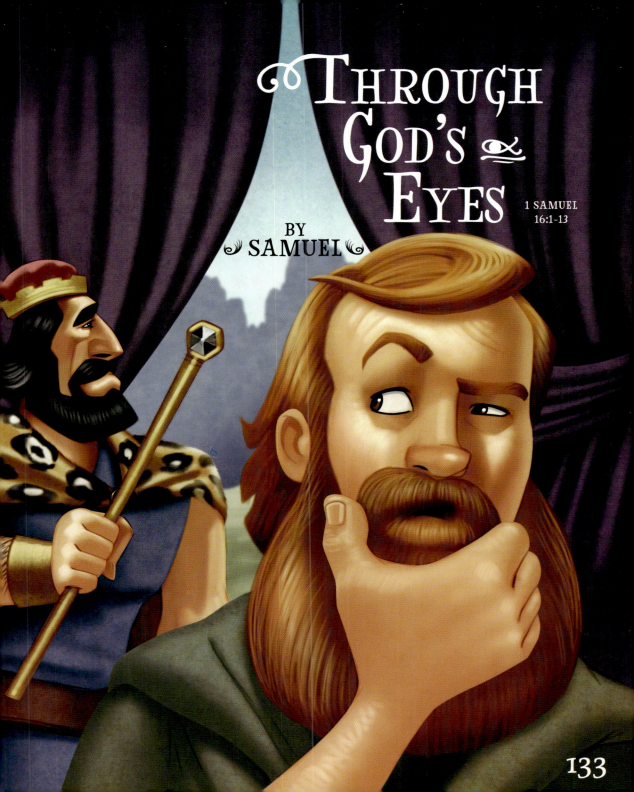

Through God's Eyes

by Samuel

1 SAMUEL 16:1-13

I wish I could tell you that all of Israel's kings were good, but some of them were awful. They didn't do what God wanted. Saul was a king like that, and God wanted me to find a new king.

"Go to Bethlehem and talk to Jesse. One of his sons will be the new king," God told me.

But I was afraid. What if Saul found out? He might kill me! Everybody knows he has a bit of a bad temper.

But I did what God told me. I went to Bethlehem. Then I invited Jesse and his sons to join me in worshipping God. Jesse's sons were big and strong.

I knew right away that one of these seven strong fellows would make a great king.

God saw things differently, though. "Don't pay attention to what they look like," God said. "I only care about what's in their heart."

One by one I looked at each of Jesse's sons. But one by one, God said, "No, not him."

Now what was I supposed to do? I felt kind of silly standing there. But then I had an idea.

"DO you have any other sons?" I asked.

"Yes, but..." said Jesse, "...but he's just the youngest of the boys. His name is David. He's out in the fields with the sheep and the goats."

"I need to see him, too," I said.

When David arrived, I saw that he was a handsome young man with beautiful eyes. He didn't look like a king to me, but God knew what he was like on the inside. God said, "This is the one. Anoint him."

(Whew! What a relief!)

136

"He's the one!" I said.

Right then and there I took some special oil and poured it on David's head. God's Spirit came upon him in a powerful way that day, and I had a feeling he was going to make a great king.

You know, that day with Jesse and his sons I learned something. There are different ways of looking at people. We usually look at their outside. That's pretty easy. But God looks at people on the inside: at who they *really* are.

People tend to view things with just their eyes. We like to judge people by how they look.

But God has a different view. God sees what's in our hearts. And that's what really matters most.

How can we see people on the inside? We can get to know them! We can listen to them and hear their stories. Pretty soon we can discover who they are on the inside.

And it's fun! Here's a challenge for you: Find someone you don't know very well—maybe a friend at school or in your neighborhood. Ask that person to tell you about a favorite thing. Now you're getting to know what that person is like on the inside!

SAMUEL

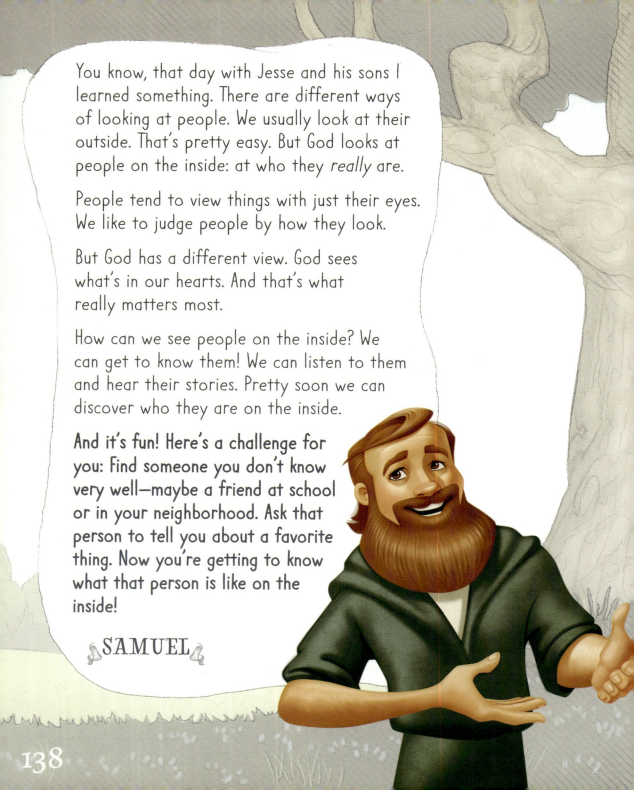

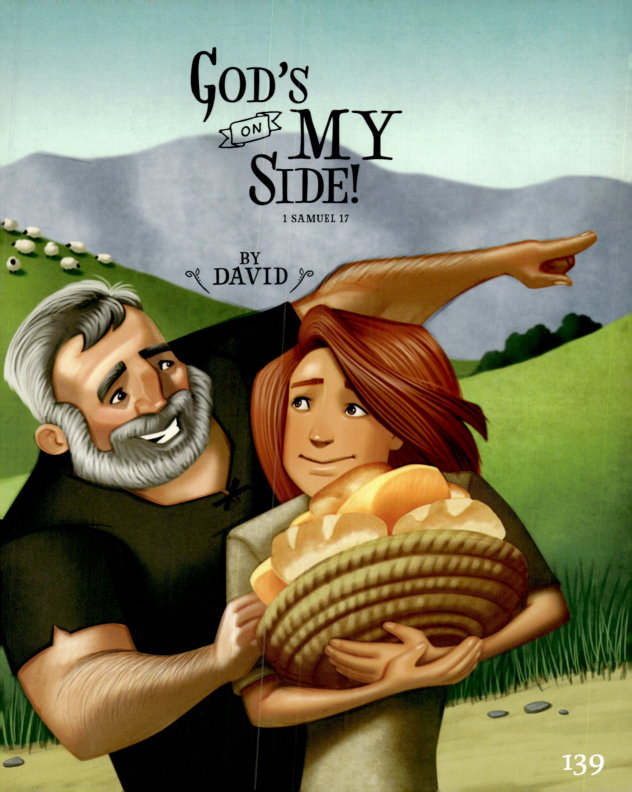

God's on My Side!

1 SAMUEL 17

BY DAVID

IT'S not easy being the youngest in the family. While my older brothers all get to go on exciting adventures, I get left behind doing the boring stuff like watching the sheep. Sheep don't do much; they just stand around eating grass all day long. Boring.

That's why I was excited when my dad asked me to take some bread and grain to my brothers. They were soldiers in Saul's army, facing an enemy called the Philistines. The Philistines bragged about their fierce warrior named Goliath—he was over nine feet tall. That's HUGE!

Every day he challenged our mightiest fighters to a battle, but no one was brave enough to face him. Even King Saul was afraid of that big bully.

My dad loaded up the bread and grain and said, "David, take this food to your brothers. Then come back here and tell me how they're doing." He sounded very worried.

When I got to my brothers, they were scared to death. In fact, every soldier in our army was terrified. For the fortieth day in a row, Goliath taunted us and defied our God. Our army just quivered in their boots.

I couldn't believe it. No one was stronger than God! God would give us the strength to fight.

SO I went straight to King Saul and told him I would fight Goliath.

"No way!" said Saul. "You're just a shrimpy kid. That bully will squash you like a bug!"

But I wasn't afraid. I knew God was on our side. Saul gave me his own heavy armor for protection, but I didn't need it. God would be my armor.

I grabbed my sling and a few smooth stones from the stream. Then I marched out to face the giant. Up close, he was even gianter than I imagined. Just one of his legs was taller than my whole body!

Still, I wasn't afraid.

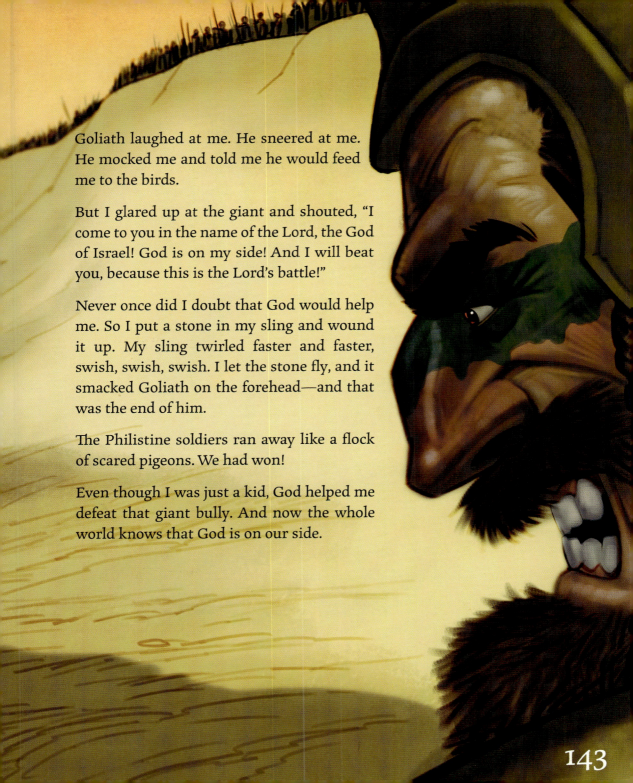

Goliath laughed at me. He sneered at me. He mocked me and told me he would feed me to the birds.

But I glared up at the giant and shouted, "I come to you in the name of the Lord, the God of Israel! God is on my side! And I will beat you, because this is the Lord's battle!"

Never once did I doubt that God would help me. So I put a stone in my sling and wound it up. My sling twirled faster and faster, swish, swish, swish. I let the stone fly, and it smacked Goliath on the forehead—and that was the end of him.

The Philistine soldiers ran away like a flock of scared pigeons. We had won!

Even though I was just a kid, God helped me defeat that giant bully. And now the whole world knows that God is on our side.

I wasn't afraid to face Goliath because I knew God was with me. Everyone else was afraid—my brothers, the soldiers, and even King Saul. They forgot that God was on their side.

You may not ever fight a giant like Goliath the way I did. But you face other "Goliaths" in life that might scare you. Remember that God is always on your side. Even when it seems like everyone else is afraid, you don't have to be.

What can you say when you're afraid? What can you say that makes you feel brave? Write down one or two things you can say to remind yourself that God is on your side.

DAVID

144

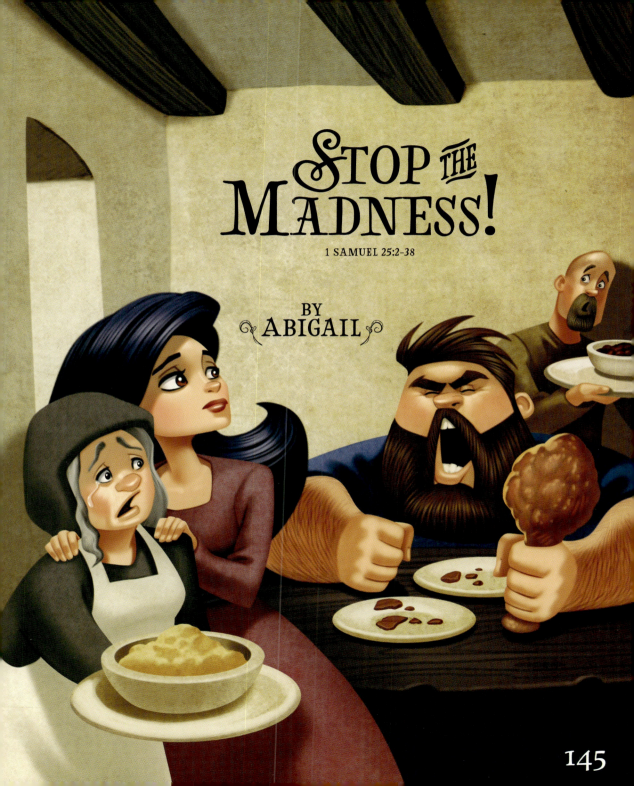

Stop the Madness!

1 SAMUEL 25:2-38

BY ABIGAIL

MY husband, Nabal, is not the nicest person in the world. To tell you the truth, he's a bit of a grump. Actually, he's a big fool.

And I can tell you right now this story doesn't end well for him.

It was sheep-shearing time, and David sent ten of his men to take a message of peace and blessings to Nabal. They asked Nabal if he had any extra food and supplies he could let them have, since David's men had always been good to us. They helped our family and protected our sheep.

What a lovely thing to do, right?

Nabal didn't think so. In fact, it just made him angry. He yelled at those kind young men and called them names. He even had a few nasty things to say about David. What a bully!

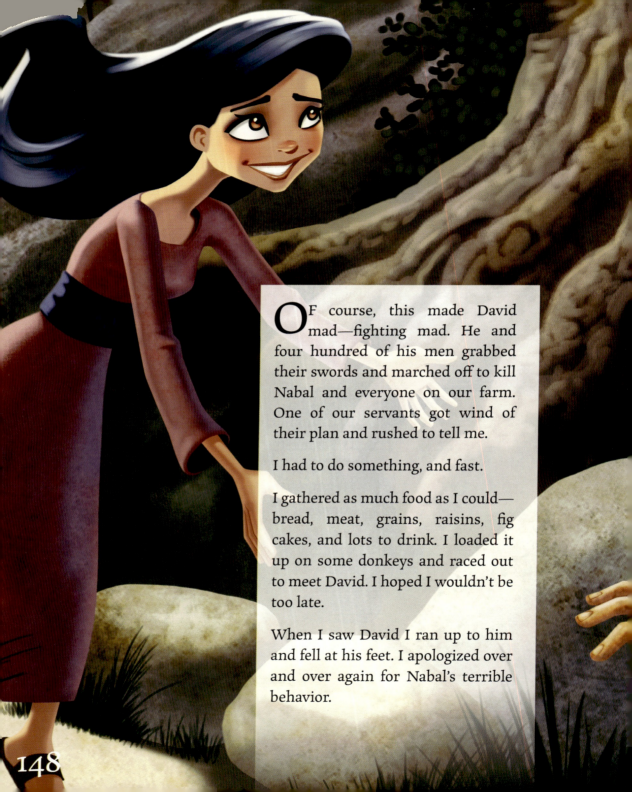

OF course, this made David mad—fighting mad. He and four hundred of his men grabbed their swords and marched off to kill Nabal and everyone on our farm. One of our servants got wind of their plan and rushed to tell me.

I had to do something, and fast.

I gathered as much food as I could—bread, meat, grains, raisins, fig cakes, and lots to drink. I loaded it up on some donkeys and raced out to meet David. I hoped I wouldn't be too late.

When I saw David I ran up to him and fell at his feet. I apologized over and over again for Nabal's terrible behavior.

"Don't pay any attention to my husband. He's a fool!" I said. "But please don't murder him. You're a good man, David. If you kill Nabal, it'll put a blemish on your record as a great man of God."

David nodded. "Wow, I think you're right. Thank you for bringing me to my senses! I had gotten pretty angry myself, and I'm glad you helped me calm down," he said, and sent me home in peace.

But things got worse for Nabal. When I told him what had happened, the shock paralyzed him. And that nasty old grouch died ten days later.

You know, it was kind of sad about my husband. He never got to experience the joy of being kind. Even when others tried to be kind to him, he lashed out in anger. That's no way to live your life.

We all get angry sometimes, and that's okay. But God wants us to control our anger. Being friends with God means loving people the way God loves them. And we can't love people when we're angry all the time.

I'd rather be at peace with people. That's how I want to spend my life: being a peacemaker.

You know, it's easy to be kind! Find someone today and tell that person one thing you really like about him or her.

ABIGAIL

Just One Wish

1 KINGS 3; PROVERBS 1:1-7; 2:1-22

BY SOLOMON

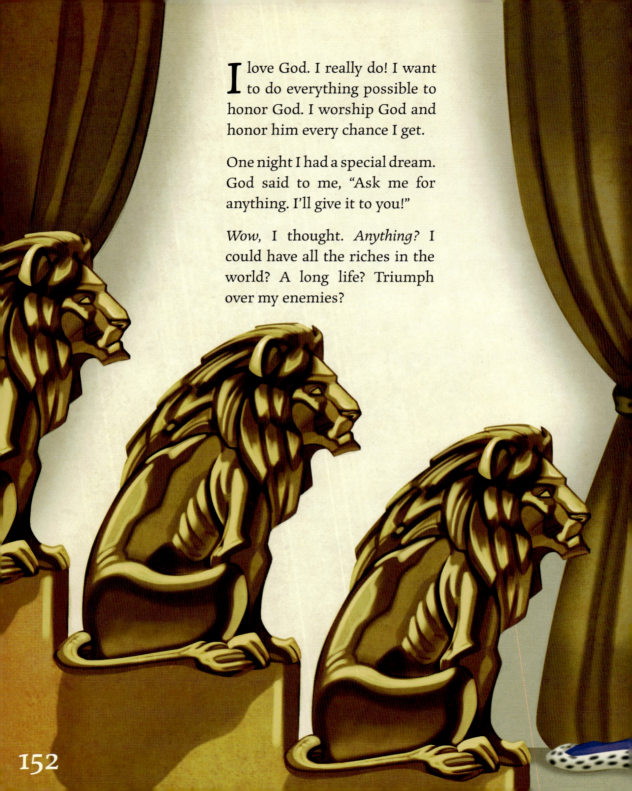

I love God. I really do! I want to do everything possible to honor God. I worship God and honor him every chance I get.

One night I had a special dream. God said to me, "Ask me for anything. I'll give it to you!"

Wow, I thought. *Anything?* I could have all the riches in the world? A long life? Triumph over my enemies?

God has been so good to me and my family, especially my father, King David. I wanted to honor God by being a good ruler for his people. But I honestly don't feel like I know what I'm doing half the time, so my answer to God was easy.

I asked for wisdom.

That made God happy. God made me the wisest man in the world. But he also gave me so much more—riches, fame, and power, too.

GOD'S wisdom has served me well. Just the other day two women came to me to settle an awful argument. They were holding a baby, and both were *very* upset.

"Her baby died, and she swapped it with my newborn baby!" sobbed the first woman.

"No way!" shouted the other woman. "It was her own baby that died!"

It was an impossible situation, but God's wisdom helped me solve the mystery.

It sounds terrible, but I told them to cut the baby in half; then I'd give them each a half.

"Fine!" snorted the second woman.

"NO!" cried the first woman. "Please don't hurt him. She can have the baby!"

Clearly the baby belonged to the first woman. She cared so much about her child and she wanted him to live. So I gave the baby to his true mother.

155

Take it from me, wisdom is better than any other treasure in the world. My kingdom prospered because God's wisdom guided the decisions I made.

Being wise doesn't guarantee that you'll be rich, or famous, or powerful. But wisdom is free. And God loves us so much that he'll give it to us when we ask for it.

One of the best ways to get wisdom is by reading God's Word. You're doing that right now. Way to go! God speaks to us through the Bible and can help us understand how to grow in a friendship with him.

Try it! Read the Bible every night before you go to bed.

❦—SOLOMON—❦

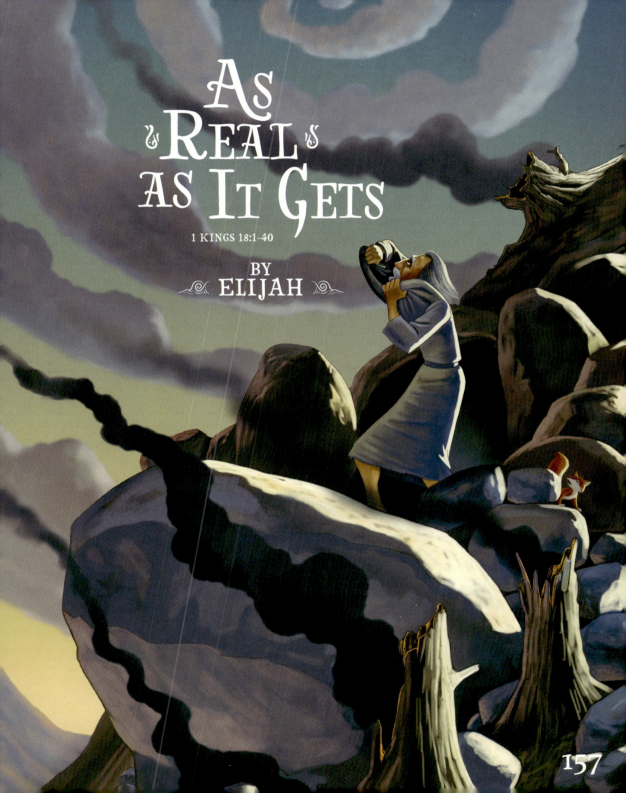

As Real As It Gets

1 KINGS 18:1-40

BY ELIJAH

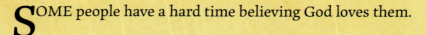

SOME people have a hard time believing God loves them.

But not me! God has taken care of me through some really hard times. When I was hiding from mean King Ahab in the desert, God even sent ravens to bring me food every day. Ravens are birds, kind of like crows. To think God showed his love for me through birds!

But I couldn't avoid Ahab forever. Even though that troublemaker wanted to kill me, God sent me to prove to him that God was real—and that Ahab's fake gods were, well, fake.

I met Ahab on Mount Carmel for a major showdown. He brought four hundred and fifty of his prophets of Baal. (Baal was the fake god Ahab chose to follow instead of the one true God.) I told Ahab's prophets to build an altar to Baal while I built my own altar to God.

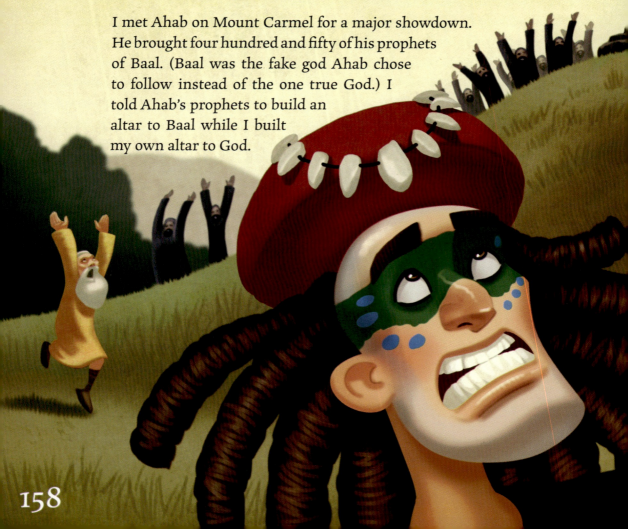

"The god who brings fire to an altar is the one true God!" I said. "If Baal is God, then follow him. But if the Lord is God, then you must follow him!"

Those poor prophets of Baal tried and tried and tried and tried to get Baal to send fire. They danced and hollered like a bunch of fools. I told them to yell louder, but it didn't help.

I poked fun at them because I knew nothing would happen. "Maybe Baal went on vacation! Maybe he's asleep! Maybe he's out going to the bathroom!"

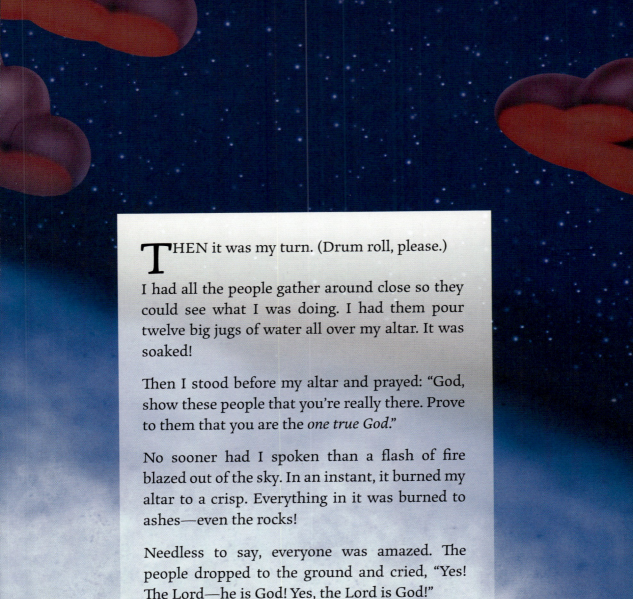

THEN it was my turn. (Drum roll, please.)

I had all the people gather around close so they could see what I was doing. I had them pour twelve big jugs of water all over my altar. It was soaked!

Then I stood before my altar and prayed: "God, show these people that you're really there. Prove to them that you are the *one true God*."

No sooner had I spoken than a flash of fire blazed out of the sky. In an instant, it burned my altar to a crisp. Everything in it was burned to ashes—even the rocks!

Needless to say, everyone was amazed. The people dropped to the ground and cried, "Yes! The Lord—he is God! Yes, the Lord is God!"

Yes! Yes, he is.

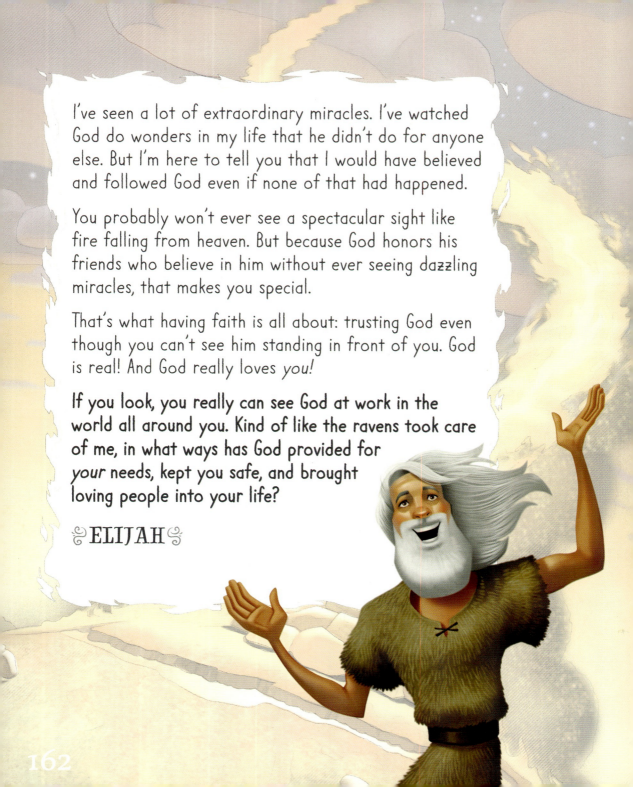

I've seen a lot of extraordinary miracles. I've watched God do wonders in my life that he didn't do for anyone else. But I'm here to tell you that I would have believed and followed God even if none of that had happened.

You probably won't ever see a spectacular sight like fire falling from heaven. But because God honors his friends who believe in him without ever seeing dazzling miracles, that makes you special.

That's what having faith is all about: trusting God even though you can't see him standing in front of you. God is real! And God really loves *you!*

If you look, you really can see God at work in the world all around you. Kind of like the ravens took care of me, in what ways has God provided for *your* needs, kept you safe, and brought loving people into your life?

❧ELIJAH❧

Let It Flow, Let It Flow, Let It Flow

2 KINGS 4:1-7

BY ELISHA

I think God kind of likes surprises. You never know what creative new way God is going to use to give you what you need!

Take this poor widow I just met. Her husband died and left her with a lot of debt. The banker wanted his money, and soon he even threatened to take her two sons and sell them as slaves. But she was broke. All she had was one little jar of olive oil.

So she asked me for help. I knew God would come to her rescue.

I told her to borrow as many jars as she could find: from friends, neighbors, anyone who had an extra jar or two sitting around. Then I told her to pour the oil from her one jar into all the empty jars.

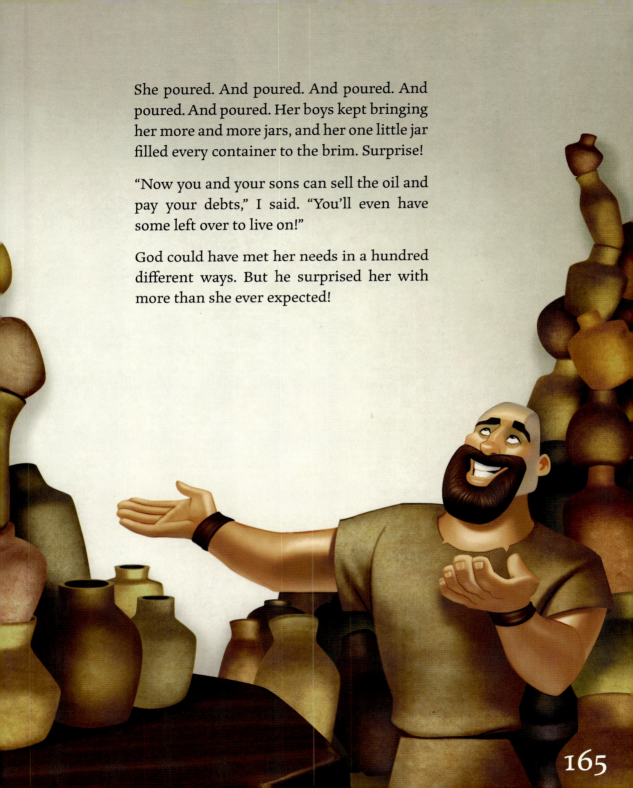

She poured. And poured. And poured. And poured. And poured. Her boys kept bringing her more and more jars, and her one little jar filled every container to the brim. Surprise!

"Now you and your sons can sell the oil and pay your debts," I said. "You'll even have some left over to live on!"

God could have met her needs in a hundred different ways. But he surprised her with more than she ever expected!

Don't you love happy endings? That one little jar of oil turned into a fountain of joy for that poor widow and her boys.

God's love works the same way! God keeps pouring his love into your life and it never runs out.

God met that widow's needs, and God meets *your* needs, too. Name some of the needs you have in your family. Then pray to God and ask for help. You might be surprised by what God does!

ELISHA

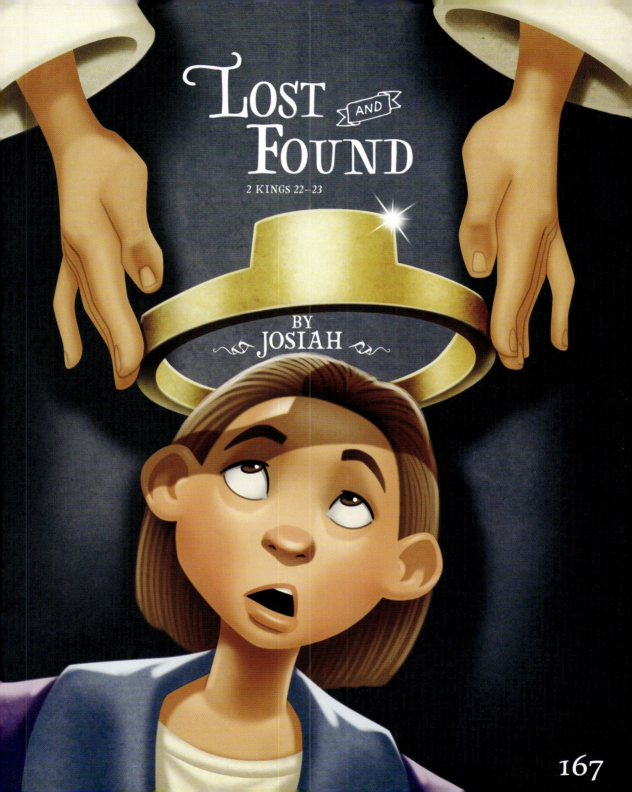

LOST AND FOUND

2 KINGS 22–23

BY JOSIAH

IMAGINE if you got to be in charge of everything. You could make all the rules, boss everyone around, and do whatever you wanted to do.

That's exactly what happened to me. I became king of Israel when I was eight years old! That's a lot of power for a little kid like me. But even though I could do whatever I chose, there was one thing I wanted to do more than anything else: honor God.

When I was older, I started a plan to restore God's Temple, the building where the people worshipped God. No one had used it for years and years, and it was a dusty, dirty mess.

While the people were fixing the Temple, the priest found a scroll inside that had all of God's rules. It had been lost and forgotten for who knows how long.

My secretary read it to me, and I couldn't believe what I was hearing. Yikes! My people had not been obeying God the way we were supposed to. This scroll told us that God was so angry he was going to punish us—badly.

I was so upset! I cried and tore my clothes. What could we do?

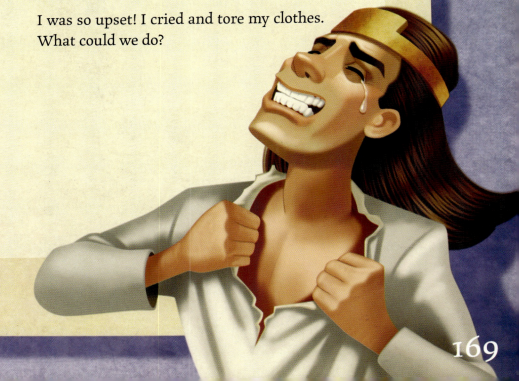

RIGHT away I sent my officials to talk with the prophet Huldah. She was wise, and I hoped she might help us.

She said that because I was sorry, and since I was truly sad when I heard the news, God would not punish us during my lifetime.

God had helped me discover his Scriptures. Now I knew what I needed to do.

I brought all the people together and read all of God's rules. Then I pledged to obey God for the rest of my life. I destroyed all the altars, shrines, and idols to all the fake gods. I cleaned house!

Now God's rules were our rules. The Lord was our God. And I spent the rest of my days as king loving and honoring God the way he wanted us to in the first place.

Being a king is harder than you think. And being a kid king is even harder! All along I knew I couldn't do a good job without God's help.

I never read God's holy Scriptures until I was twenty-six years old. But once I had read them, I knew I needed to obey them.

And now I'm close to God. I listen to God, pray to God, worship God, and think about God all day. I know God loves me and will always be my friend.

Growing close to God is way better than being a king. So I try to stay close to God by reading his book—the Bible—every day. You can, too! Try to read one of God's stories every day.

⚜ JOSIAH ⚜

HOME AT LAST

EZRA 3:1-13; 7:1-10;
9:6—10:17

BY EZRA

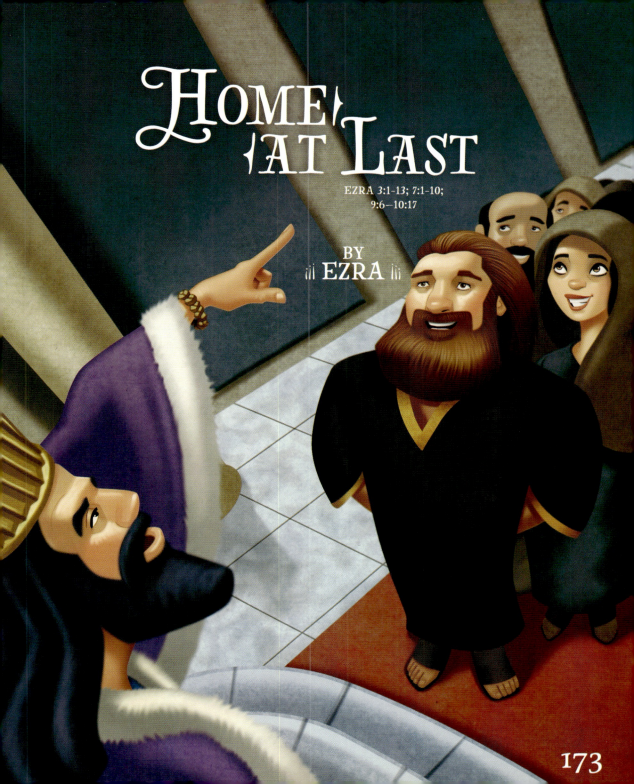

IT was an exciting time to be part of God's people! We had been living as slaves in Babylon for seventy years when King Cyrus decided it was time for us to return home to Jerusalem.

One of the first things we wanted to do was rebuild the Temple, the building where we worshipped God. The first group to go back to Jerusalem got the project going. They bought giant cedar logs and floated them down the coast from Lebanon.

They got busy rebuilding the altar and the Temple's foundation. Everyone was feeling happy again. They paused to thank God and celebrate. The priests blew trumpets and clashed cymbals, and all the people sang a song that went something like this:

"God is so good! God's love lasts forever!"

They shouted and wept, and then wept and shouted some more. Their sweet sounds could be heard for miles.

175

AFTER the Temple was finished, I traveled with a second group to Jerusalem. Our people had rebuilt the Temple, and now it was time for me to rebuild our people by teaching them about God.

With the Temple finished and our people growing closer to God again, we wanted to throw a party.

But not just any party. Our people hadn't felt this much joy in a long, long time. We dedicated the new Temple to God with hundreds of offerings. Once again, we had a place of our own where we could worship God together, just like the old days.

We were home!

One of the best things in life is celebration. Of course, every day we have so much to be thankful for. But sometimes it's good for us to sing a little louder, laugh a little longer, and hug a little tighter.

My people were so happy to be back in our home again. Seventy years is a long time to be away from home. We knew it was a special time in our history.

The most important thing about our celebration, though, is that it focused on God. We thanked God, we worshipped God, and we honored God with everything we had. God had shown his love to us again.

Put yourself in my shoes... er, sandals. How do *you* think it would feel to return home after being away for a long, long time? What's the first thing you would do? How would you thank God?

EZRA

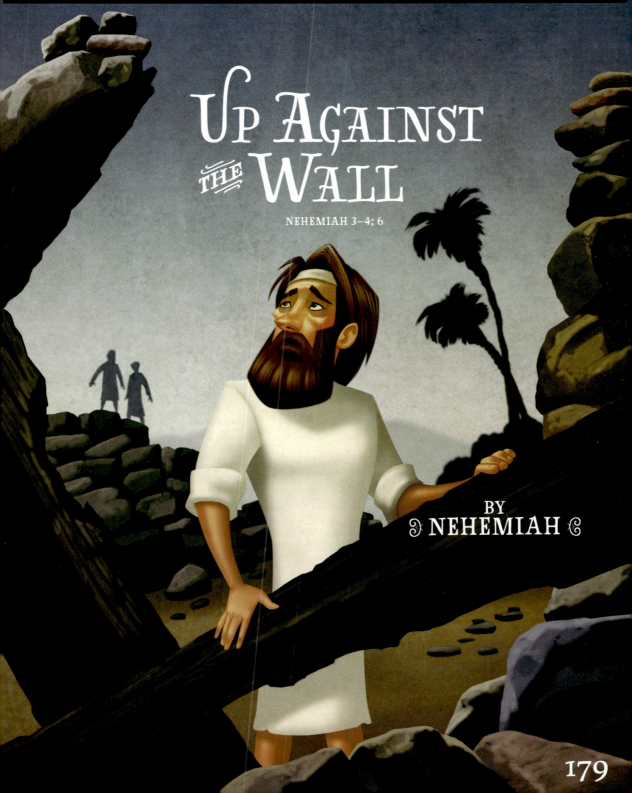

Up Against the Wall

Nehemiah 3–4; 6

by Nehemiah

WE had returned to Jerusalem. We had rebuilt God's Temple. Now it was time to give our home some protection.

Cities in our time needed walls to protect us from our enemies. Unfortunately, we had a lot of enemies. Fortunately, God was not one of them. God was our friend.

The wall around Jerusalem had been destroyed and burned a long time ago. So we put different groups of people to work on sections of the wall and its gates. It was a BIG JOB.

It wasn't easy. And our enemies didn't like it. In fact, they were mad! They mocked us, saying stuff like, "That wall would fall over if even a fox walked on top of it!"

Things got so bad that I placed armed guards all along the wall where the people were working. If anyone attacked, we'd be ready.

But even with guards all around, I prayed that God would protect us.

THE longer we worked, the angrier our enemies became. They made up lies about us. They threatened to hurt us again and again. They even tried to lure me out of the city so they could kill me!

But we wouldn't be stopped. I wasn't afraid. After all, God was with us. Running away would show that I didn't trust God to protect us.

Instead of bowing to our enemies, we kept right on working. We stayed faithful to God brick by brick, beam by beam, nail by nail.

Not only did God protect us, but he also helped us work fast, too. We finished that wall in just fifty-two days. Imagine that—the entire wall rebuilt around the whole city of Jerusalem in less than two months. Thanks be to God!

Now our enemies weren't angry—they were frightened! They could see that God was with us.

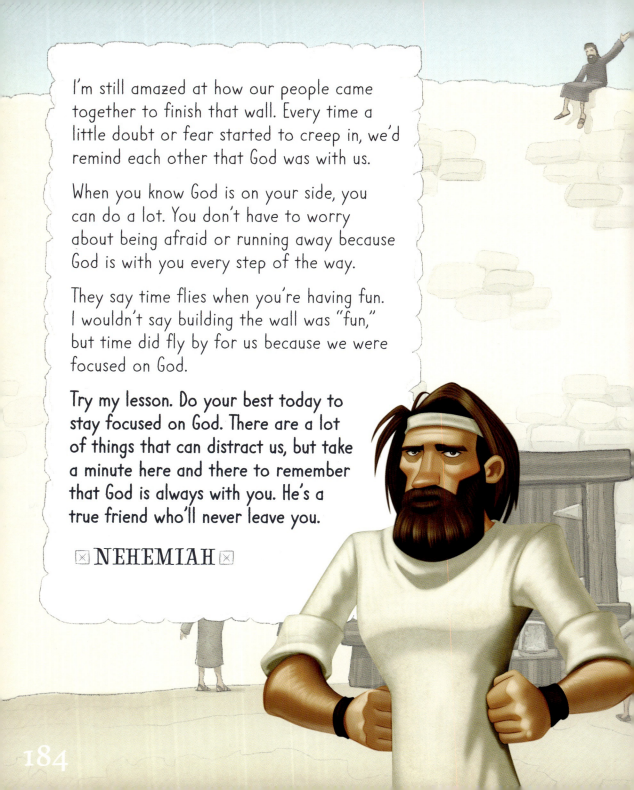

I'm still amazed at how our people came together to finish that wall. Every time a little doubt or fear started to creep in, we'd remind each other that God was with us.

When you know God is on your side, you can do a lot. You don't have to worry about being afraid or running away because God is with you every step of the way.

They say time flies when you're having fun. I wouldn't say building the wall was "fun," but time did fly by for us because we were focused on God.

Try my lesson. Do your best today to stay focused on God. There are a lot of things that can distract us, but take a minute here and there to remember that God is always with you. He's a true friend who'll never leave you.

☒ **NEHEMIAH** ☒

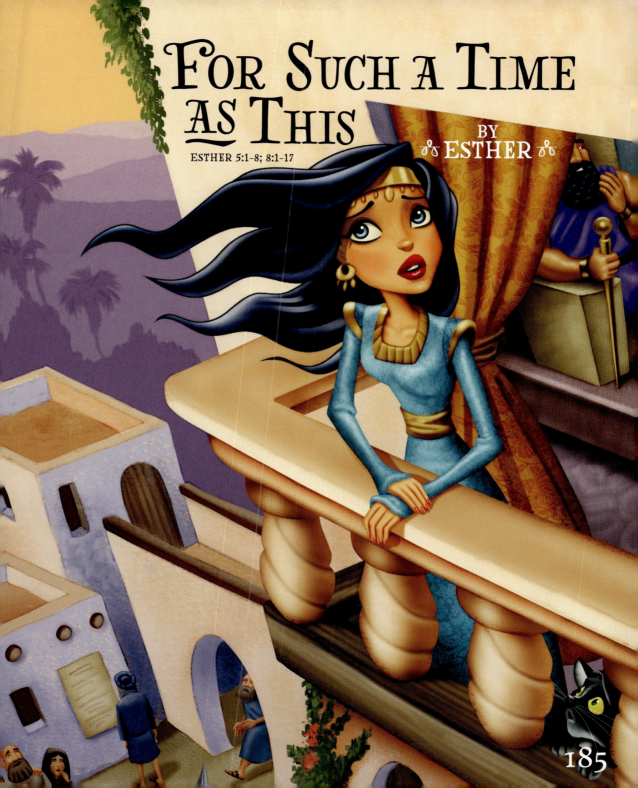

FOR SUCH A TIME AS THIS

ESTHER 5:1-8; 8:1-17

BY ❧ ESTHER ❧

185

LOTS of kids dream of being kings or queens. I'm one of the lucky few—I actually got to *be* a queen! But it wasn't really luck, and it wasn't for any reason I ever expected.

I was just a girl when it all started. I was living with my cousin Mordecai, who had adopted me and raised me like his own daughter. We were Jews, which meant life wasn't always easy for us.

One day, King Xerxes decided to find a new queen. Lots of girls tried out, but the king chose me! Xerxes treated me better than I could have imagined. My life was filled with the most delicious feasts, the sweetest perfumes, the fanciest clothes, and the most brilliant jewels.

But there were some problems. I didn't tell the king I was a Jew because Mordecai told me to keep it a secret. On top of that, King Xerxes' right-hand man, Haman, hated my cousin Mordecai because Mordecai refused to bow down to Haman. So that scoundrel Haman hatched a plot to trick the king into ordering all Jews to be killed.

Every last one of us—including me.

Mordecai told me to talk to Xerxes right away and plead for the Jews. But it was risky. I could be killed. Yet if I didn't try, then all the Jews—my people—would die for sure.

I was so scared! I didn't know what to do. But Mordecai helped me make up my mind. He said, "Maybe you were made queen for such a time as this?"

That was all I needed to hear. I had to try.

I invited Xerxes and Haman to a fancy dinner. Haman thought it was quite an honor to be invited to eat with the king and queen. Little did he know what was about to happen.

The king started the meal by asking what I wanted. "I'll give you anything," he said, "even if it's half of my kingdom!"

"I have just one request," I said. "Would you please spare my life and the lives of my people, the Jews? Someone has paid to have us all killed."

Xerxes turned red with anger. "Who would do such a terrible thing like that?" he asked. "Who would dare to hurt the queen?"

I pointed at Haman. "*He's* our enemy, my king," I said.

Haman was dead before bedtime.

Not only were my people safe, but the king also made Mordecai his new right-hand man. Xerxes gave him a royal robe and a gold crown and put the king's ring on his finger.

God made sure I became the queen at just the right time. Since God loves us, he put me in just the right place to save his people from disaster.

189

When the king chose me to be his queen, I had no idea what was going to happen. Xerxes thought I was beautiful, and he really liked me. It was a strange new royal world I was living in, and I wasn't sure what made *me* so special.

But God knew what was going to happen. God placed me there for one reason: to protect his people.

That happens to people a lot. They find themselves in situations where they're not comfortable, or where they feel they don't belong, or where they have no idea what's going on. But God always knows our future. God puts us in the places he knows we're supposed to be.

Who knows what God may have in store for *you*? You, too, may get the chance to do something special.

ESTHER

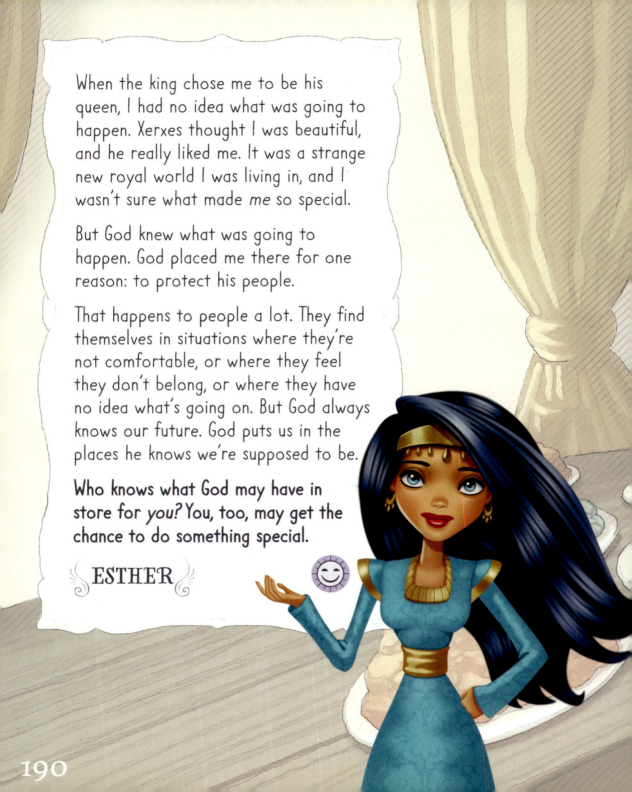

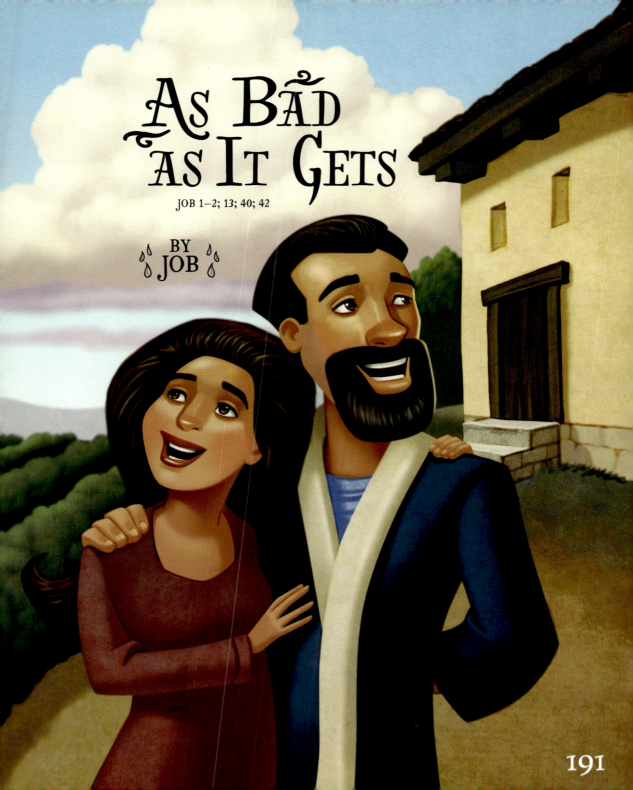

As Bad as It Gets

JOB 1–2; 13; 40; 42

BY JOB

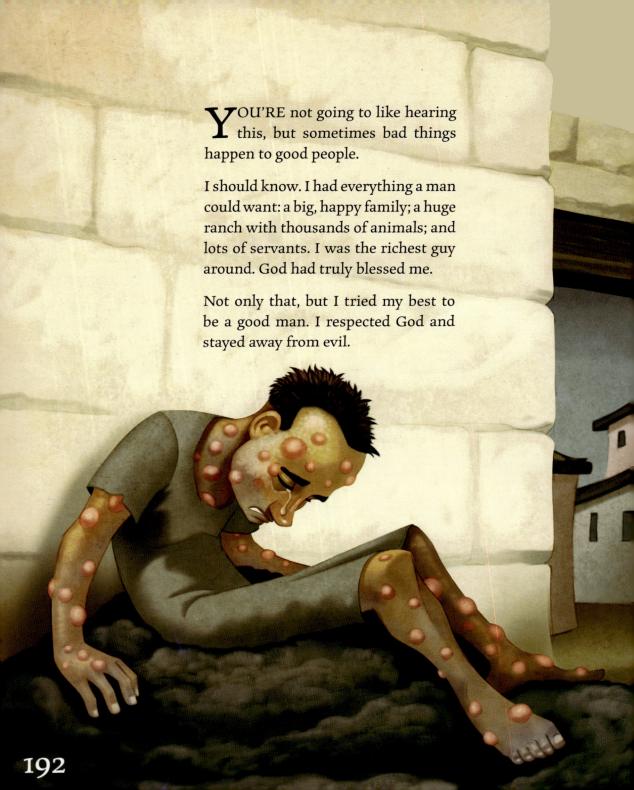

YOU'RE not going to like hearing this, but sometimes bad things happen to good people.

I should know. I had everything a man could want: a big, happy family; a huge ranch with thousands of animals; and lots of servants. I was the richest guy around. God had truly blessed me.

Not only that, but I tried my best to be a good man. I respected God and stayed away from evil.

192

Then one day, in a matter of minutes, I lost nearly everything. All of my animals were killed or stolen. Almost all of my servants died. Worst of all, my ten children were killed in a freak windstorm.

It was terrible. I fell to the ground and wept. But I didn't blame God.

That wasn't the end of it, though. Soon things got even worse. My body was covered with painful, burning, oozing sores. It was utter torture.

My wife told me to curse God and just give up on life.

But I still respected God. That's all that mattered to me.

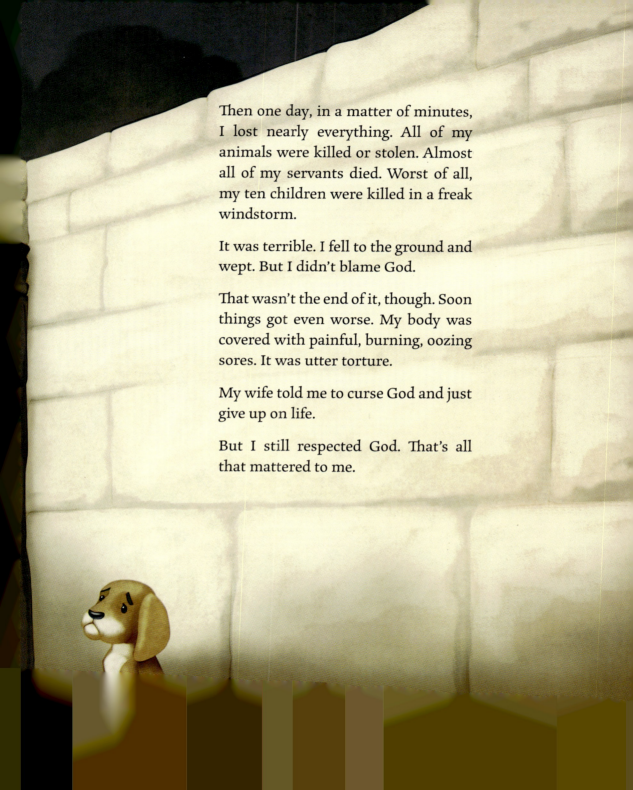

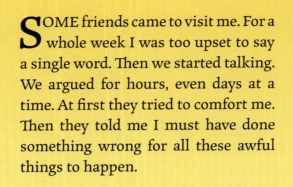

SOME friends came to visit me. For a whole week I was too upset to say a single word. Then we started talking. We argued for hours, even days at a time. At first they tried to comfort me. Then they told me I must have done something wrong for all these awful things to happen.

If I had done anything bad, I wanted to know about it so I could say I was sorry. But in the end I knew I wasn't being punished. I was suffering because... suffering happens to everyone. It's part of life. Why? I can't say.

It's more than a human like me can really understand. God alone knows all the answers.

In all the good and all the bad, God loved me. And I loved him back.

After that, God healed my body. God also returned my fortunes—double what I had before! God even gave me ten more children, and they were the most beautiful gifts in the world.

All in all, it's been a great life. And I give God ALL the credit.

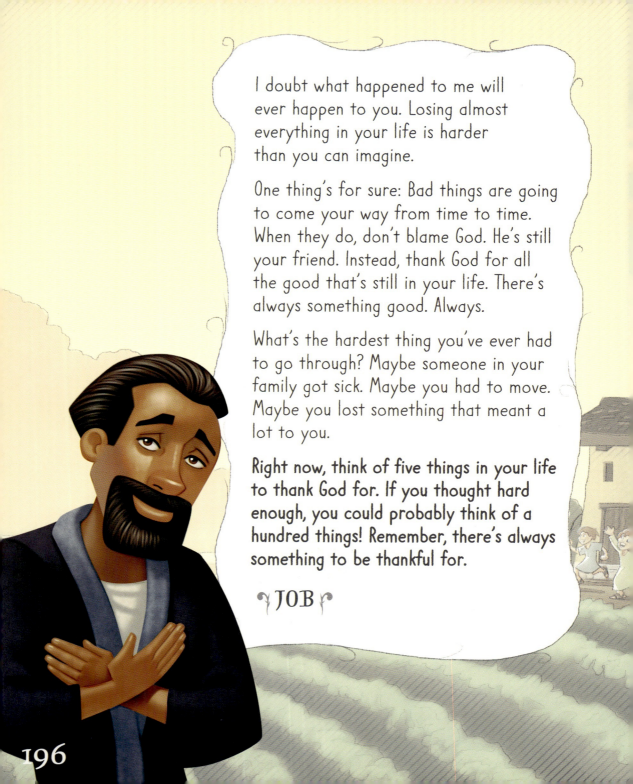

I doubt what happened to me will ever happen to you. Losing almost everything in your life is harder than you can imagine.

One thing's for sure: Bad things are going to come your way from time to time. When they do, don't blame God. He's still your friend. Instead, thank God for all the good that's still in your life. There's always something good. Always.

What's the hardest thing you've ever had to go through? Maybe someone in your family got sick. Maybe you had to move. Maybe you lost something that meant a lot to you.

Right now, think of five things in your life to thank God for. If you thought hard enough, you could probably think of a hundred things! Remember, there's always something to be thankful for.

ᐧ JOB ᐧ

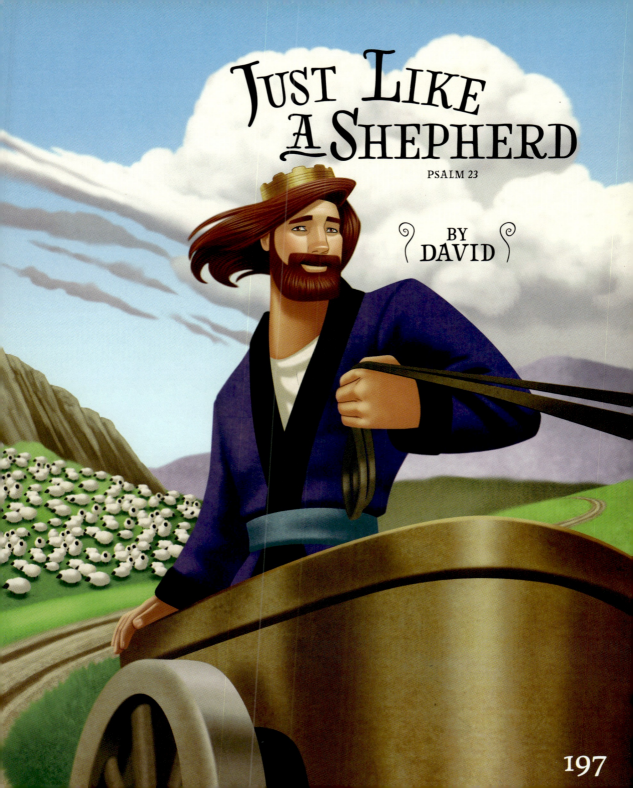

Just Like a Shepherd

PSALM 23

BY DAVID

GOD is just like a shepherd, and I'm just like his sheep.

God gives me what I need and takes me to all the best places, like green fields and peaceful streams.

God makes me strong and points me in the right direction.

God stays by my side so I'm never afraid when things get scary.

God keeps me safe and sound.

God takes care of me when others want to hurt me.

God blesses me so much more than I deserve.

God's love will go with me wherever I go, for the rest of my life.

Being one of God's sheep sounds awesome, doesn't it? I can't imagine anything better. God does it all!

Before I was a king, I was a shepherd. I cared for my sheep the best I knew how. I even fought off lions and bears to keep them safe!

Yet God is a thousand times better shepherd than I ever was. God is stronger, wiser, and bigger than anything or anyone that might come our way.

Is there anything in *your* life you're worried about right now? Let God be your shepherd. Ask God right now to take care of all your worries. He will. God loves you!

ᔰᔆ DAVID ᔆᔰ

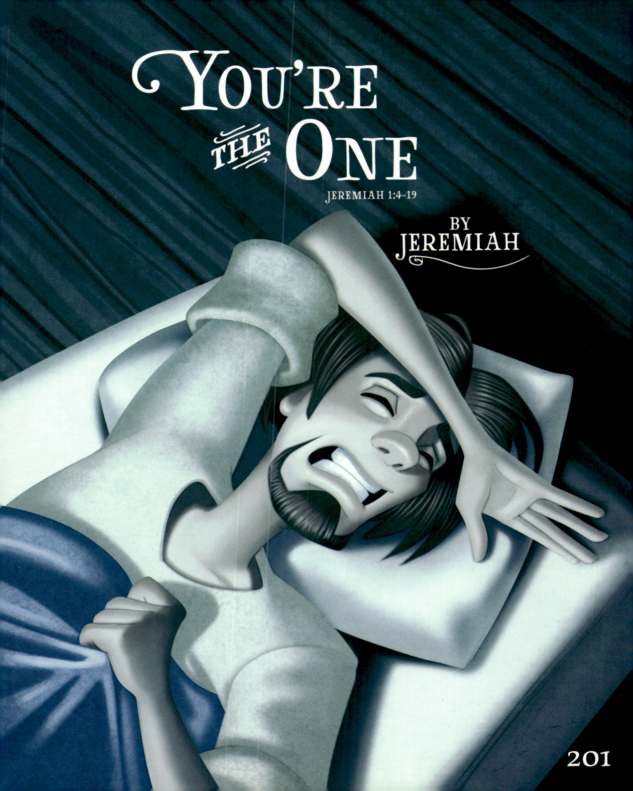

You're the One

JEREMIAH 1:4–19

BY JEREMIAH

I have a hard job. I have to tell people things they don't want to hear.

To be honest, I know how they feel. Even *I* didn't want to hear about my job when God first told me.

"I'm too young for work like that," I told God.

But, as always, God knew better. God said that, since before I was born, he had special plans for my life. God wanted me to be a prophet.

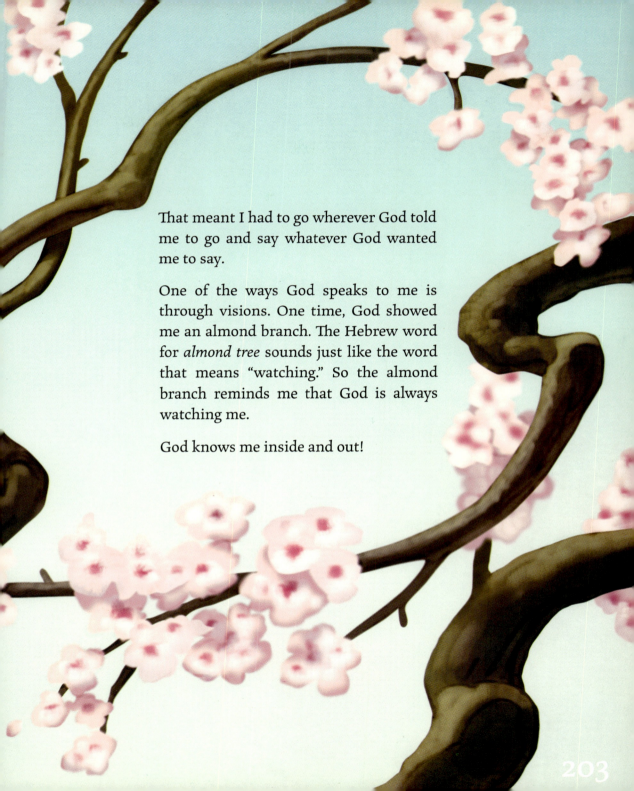

That meant I had to go wherever God told me to go and say whatever God wanted me to say.

One of the ways God speaks to me is through visions. One time, God showed me an almond branch. The Hebrew word for *almond tree* sounds just like the word that means "watching." So the almond branch reminds me that God is always watching me.

God knows me inside and out!

ANOTHER image God gave me was of boiling water spilling out of a pot. It meant that big trouble was coming for the people of Israel because they had turned their backs on God.

The Israelites weren't very happy about that news. They didn't like being in hot water! But I had to tell them anyway. It was my job.

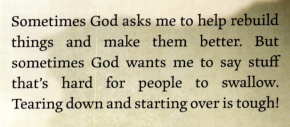

Sometimes God asks me to help rebuild things and make them better. But sometimes God wants me to say stuff that's hard for people to swallow. Tearing down and starting over is tough!

Yet God gives me strength. "Don't be afraid!" he tells me again and again. Even though I wasn't too sure about myself in the beginning, God knew I could do it.

God is a friend who knows me better than I know myself!

When I was a kid, I never dreamed of being a prophet. Prophets can be pretty unpopular. I mean, who wants to be the bearer of bad news all the time?

But that's what God made me for. God knew I'd be the best person for the job, and, as always, God was right.

God made you for something special, too! Maybe you don't know what it is yet. That's okay. God knows who you really are, and he has a plan for your life.

What's something *you're* really good at? How can you honor God with that special talent?

🌸 JEREMIAH 🌸

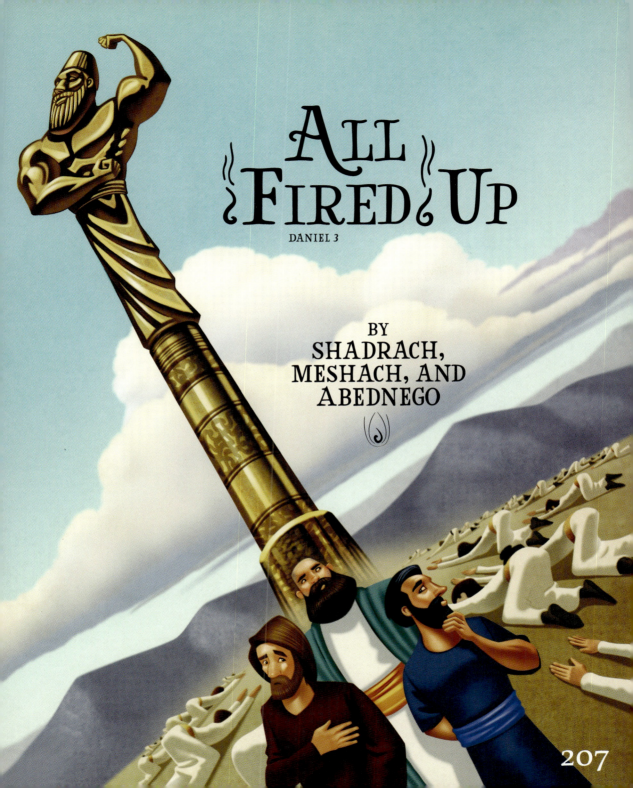

ALL FIRED UP

DANIEL 3

BY SHADRACH, MESHACH, AND ABEDNEGO

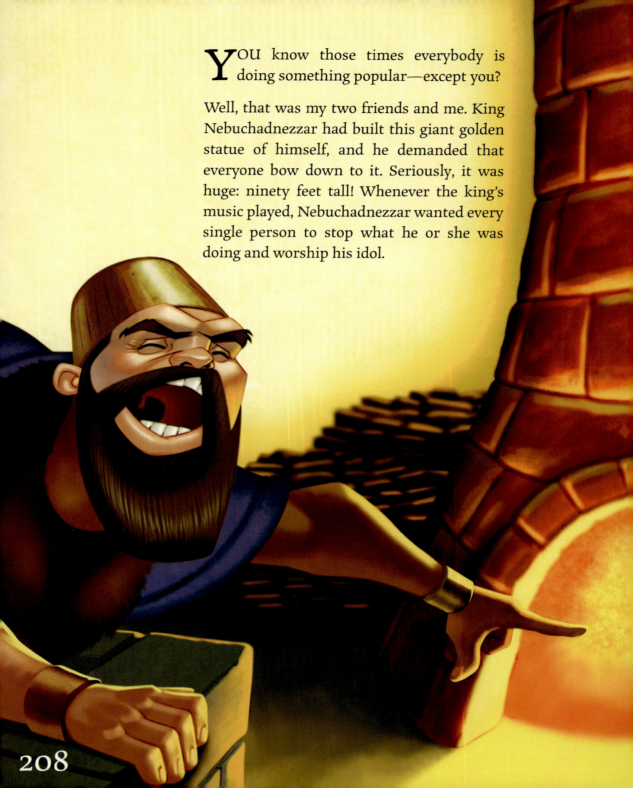

YOU know those times everybody is doing something popular—except you?

Well, that was my two friends and me. King Nebuchadnezzar had built this giant golden statue of himself, and he demanded that everyone bow down to it. Seriously, it was huge: ninety feet tall! Whenever the king's music played, Nebuchadnezzar wanted every single person to stop what he or she was doing and worship his idol.

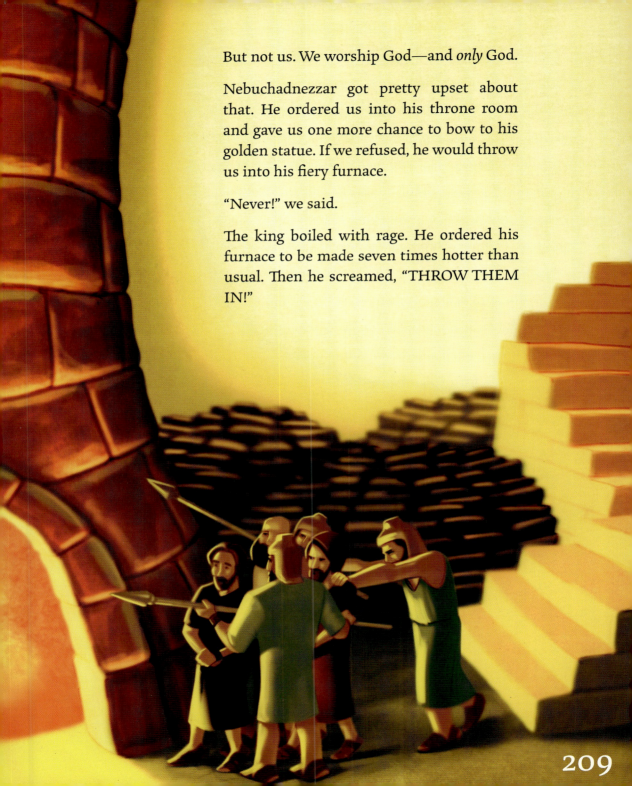

But not us. We worship God—and *only* God.

Nebuchadnezzar got pretty upset about that. He ordered us into his throne room and gave us one more chance to bow to his golden statue. If we refused, he would throw us into his fiery furnace.

"Never!" we said.

The king boiled with rage. He ordered his furnace to be made seven times hotter than usual. Then he screamed, "THROW THEM IN!"

THE fire was so hot it even killed the guards who tossed us in.

The flames swirled and flashed all around us. But we kept our cool. We knew God could save us. And even if he didn't, we knew we'd done the right thing.

When Nebuchadnezzar looked inside the furnace, he couldn't believe what he saw. Not only were we still alive, but there was also a fourth man standing with us. God had sent an angel to stand by our side!

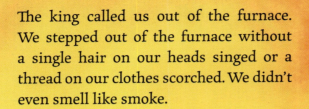

The king called us out of the furnace. We stepped out of the furnace without a single hair on our heads singed or a thread on our clothes scorched. We didn't even smell like smoke.

Nebuchadnezzar had no choice. After what he had just seen, he *had* to praise our God. Now the king's heart was on fire for the one true God. "Praise the God of Shadrach, Meshach, and Abednego!" he exclaimed.

The king was so impressed he actually promoted us to even higher positions in his kingdom. And our love for God burned as bright as ever.

Some might say this is a story about three guys. But we know better. This is a story about FOUR of us because God was with us the whole time.

It's not always easy to take a stand for what you know is right, but God will *always* stand with you.

Have you ever been tempted to join your friends in doing something you knew was wrong? What can you do to be ready to stand firm and make the right choice?

Take it from us: Sticking with God is always the best option. You'll be on fire for God, too!

SHADRACH, MESHACH, AND ABEDNEGO

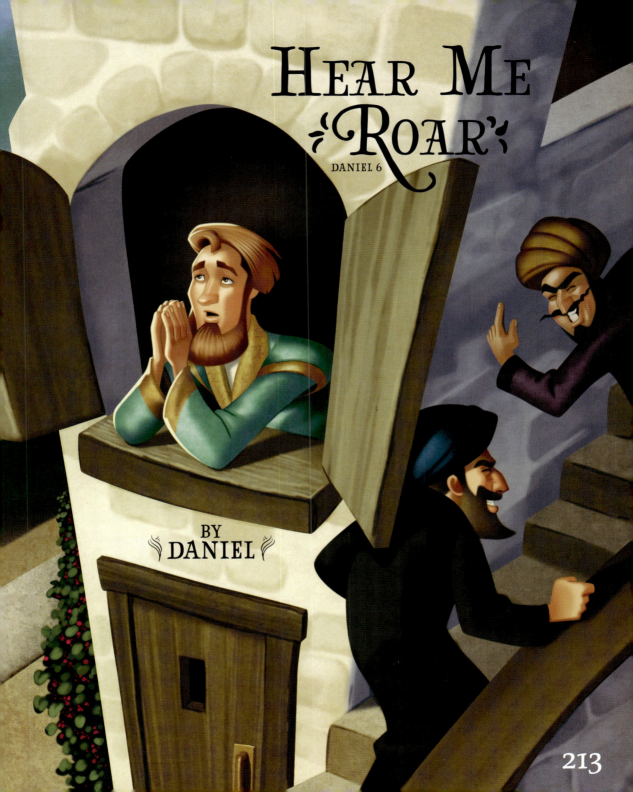

HEAR ME ROAR

DANIEL 6

BY DANIEL

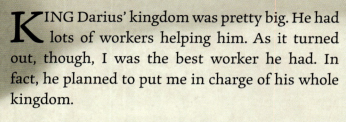

KING Darius' kingdom was pretty big. He had lots of workers helping him. As it turned out, though, I was the best worker he had. In fact, he planned to put me in charge of his whole kingdom.

His other workers didn't like that, so they plotted to take me down. But I was good. They couldn't find a single thing wrong with me. That's why I was Darius' favorite.

So they picked on the one thing they knew I would never turn my back on: my faith in God. They tricked Darius into making a law that said people could pray only to the king. If they prayed to anyone else, they'd be thrown into the lions' den for cat food!

Then the sneaky workers spied on me. No matter what the law said, I still prayed to God three times a day, looking out my window toward Jerusalem.

"Aha! We got him!" they thought. So they reported me to Darius at once. The king was deeply upset. After all, he really liked me. I was his favorite!

But King Darius had no choice. The law was the law. He would have to throw me in the lions' den.

When they lowered me into the den, the lions looked hungry. They paced back and forth, drooling and ready to pounce on their next meal: ME! The king could only shake his head. "I hope your God can rescue you," he told me.

Then they sealed the den shut.

FOR the rest of the night Darius didn't eat. He couldn't sleep at all. He was really, really worried about me.

First thing in the morning, the king rushed to the den as quickly as he could. He opened up the door and shouted, "Daniel! Are you okay? Was your God able to save you?"

"Long live the king!" I called out. "I'm safe. God shut the lions' mouths because he knows I'm innocent."

The king was thrilled! "YES!" Darius shouted, and had me lifted out right away.

King Darius arrested my accusers and threw THEM into the den. The lions finally got their dinner.

King Darius was so amazed I survived that he decided to worship my God, too. He even sent out a message to everyone in his kingdom, praising God and giving him all the glory for his love and power.

No one could have saved me from those hungry lions except God. Even King Darius knew that. It was no surprise to me that God came to my rescue.

No matter what, God never lets us down. People let us down all the time, but not God. God loves me, and God loves you, too.

When you face tough situations, do you trust God? Think about a time you were really nervous or afraid. How did God stay by your side through that time?

Next time life throws you into a hard situation, find someone to pray with you. Together, ask God to be with you. He will!

DANIEL

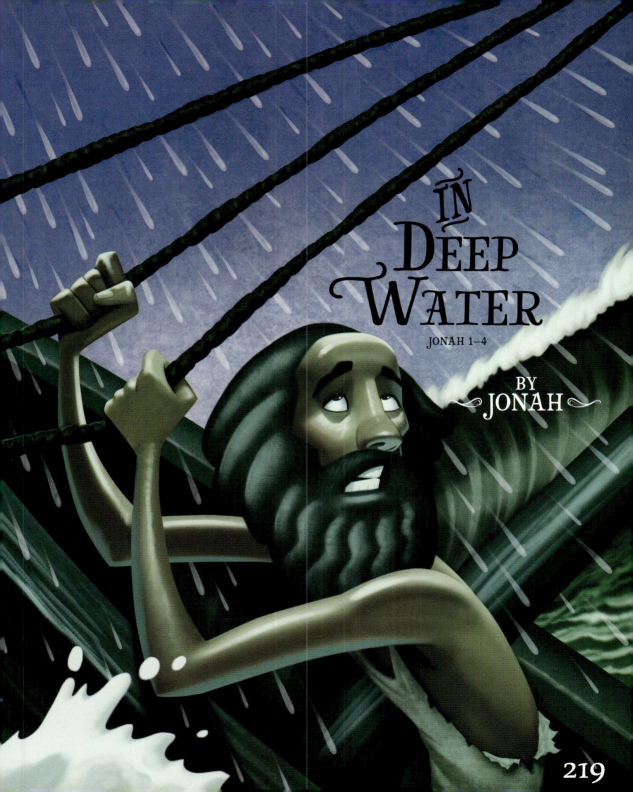

In Deep Water

JONAH 1–4

BY ~JONAH~

I wouldn't be telling you this story right now if God didn't give second chances. I'd still be fish food if he didn't. But I'm getting ahead of myself.

Since I was a prophet, I had to tell people things God wanted them to hear. And they weren't usually good things. The people of the great city of Nineveh were bad. Really bad. Downright nasty, if we're being honest. And God wanted *me* to go tell them he was going to punish them big time.

ME? No way! Not a chance! After all, when God announces his judgment, people say they're sorry and start doing the right thing again. And they don't even get punished. That's not fair! Plus, the people of Nineveh were mean. And I mean *mean*!

So I jumped on a ship—and headed in the opposite direction.

But then a huge storm hit (and I'm pretty sure God made it happen). The wind and rain and waves got worse and worse. The ship was going to sink any minute. Believe it or not, I was sound asleep down below. (Running away from God is *very* tiring!) The captain shook me awake, and when I saw the storm I had a sinking feeling.

The ship's crew realized that the storm was MY fault, because they heard I was running away from God. I told them to throw me overboard, but they didn't want to. When the storm beat down even harder, though, they made up their minds.

They tossed me into the sea. "One...two...three...heave-ho!"

Whoa!

THE second I hit the water, the storm stopped. I thought I was doomed. I began to sink. Down...down...down. Seaweed wrapped around my arms and legs. I watched my last few bubbles of air float away from me. Suddenly God sent a big fish to swallow me up.

There I was, in the belly of a giant, stinky fish. Yuck. It was time for me to rethink my life.

All I could do was pray. I had tried to run away from God, but God chased me down and saved my life. He gave me more than I deserved. I promised God next time I would do what he asked me to do.

God gave me a second chance. It was only fair that God give Nineveh a second chance, too.

Three days later that fish spat me out on the beach. Blech! This time I did what I was told and headed straight for Nineveh. I gave the people God's message—that God's judgment would doom their city soon.

And guess what happened? They turned away from the evil things they were doing! Every single one of those people in nasty Nineveh told God they were sorry—even the king himself. And then God changed his mind and decided NOT to destroy their city.

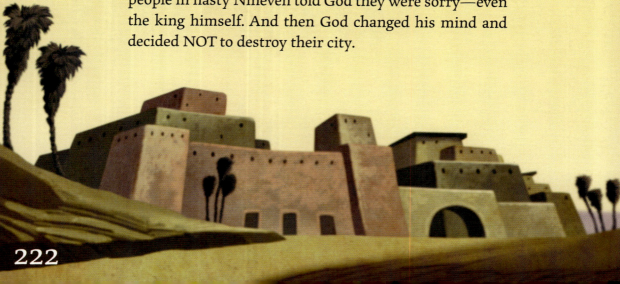

That made me mad. I didn't like those mean people from Nineveh and was hoping God would stick it to them. I trudged outside the city and sat under a little shelter, fuming. It was hot outside, and I was hot inside. But God caused a bush to grow big leaves over the shelter so I would have some cool shade. I was grateful for the plant. But the next day God let a worm eat the plant, and it shriveled up and died. I was hotheaded and mad again!

One more time, God scolded me. "Hey, Jonah, don't feel bad for a dead plant. Have compassion for the thousands of people in Nineveh who could've died!"

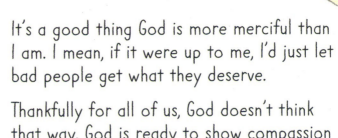

It's a good thing God is more merciful than I am. I mean, if it were up to me, I'd just let bad people get what they deserve.

Thankfully for all of us, God doesn't think that way. God is ready to show compassion and mercy to every one of us, even when we don't deserve it. *Especially* when we don't deserve it.

It can be hard for me to learn my lessons sometimes. Hopefully you're a faster learner than I am! Take it from me: Follow God's example and show love to the people you know. All people.

Who do *you* know who could use some of God's love in his or her life right now? Try saying something nice to that person.

⚜ JONAH ⚜

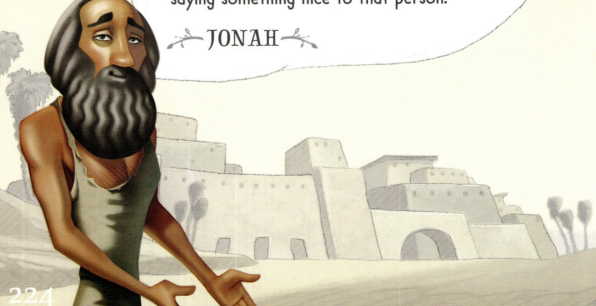

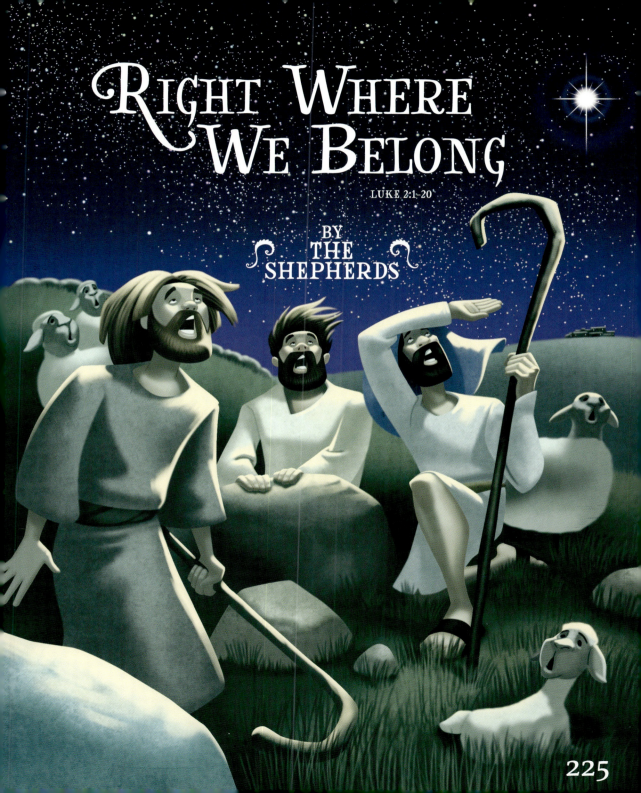

Right Where We Belong

LUKE 2:1-20

BY
THE SHEPHERDS

WE'RE just shepherds. Sure, King David was a shepherd once, but we're never going to be kings like him. We're poor. Dirty. Kinda smelly. We don't get invited to parties. We're really not all that special.

But one night—one spectacular night—we got to see the most amazing thing that ever happened.

We'd been seeing lots of families traveling from town to town, and the cities were filling up. The emperor was taking a census, and all the people had to go to their hometowns to be counted.

Not us. As people walked by, they didn't even look at us. We were just part of the scenery.

But this night was different. An angel appeared out of nowhere, right in front of us. He was blazing in a bright light. We were terrified!

"Don't be afraid," the angel said. "I have some good news for you, and it's going to make a lot of people very happy!"

The angel told us—yes, US, a bunch of poor, nobody shepherds—a very special baby had been born in Bethlehem, the town just down the hill. It was Jesus, the Messiah himself, the Lord! The angel even told us where to find him.

Then suddenly angels surrounded us; there were angels everywhere, praising God! "Glory to God in highest heaven, and peace on earth to those with whom God is pleased," they sang. We held our breath and soaked it all in. Then just like that, they were gone.

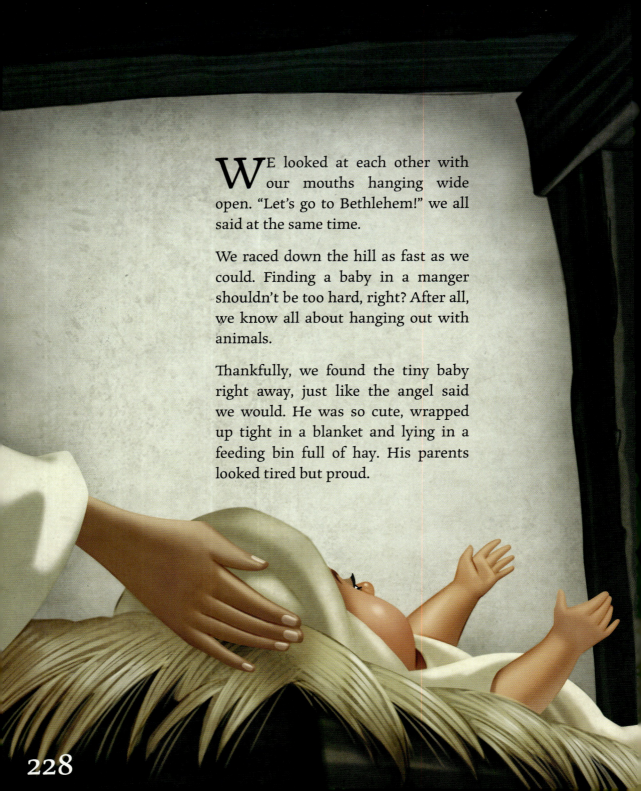

WE looked at each other with our mouths hanging wide open. "Let's go to Bethlehem!" we all said at the same time.

We raced down the hill as fast as we could. Finding a baby in a manger shouldn't be too hard, right? After all, we know all about hanging out with animals.

Thankfully, we found the tiny baby right away, just like the angel said we would. He was so cute, wrapped up tight in a blanket and lying in a feeding bin full of hay. His parents looked tired but proud.

Then we praised God, just like the angels had done.

When we left, our hearts were bursting with joy! Jesus' birth meant good news. No, GREAT news! We told everyone we met about this new gift God had given the world. We couldn't stop praising God!

And, for the first time in our lives, we felt like somebodies.

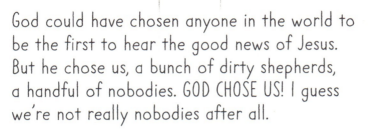

God could have chosen anyone in the world to be the first to hear the good news of Jesus. But he chose us, a bunch of dirty shepherds, a handful of nobodies. GOD CHOSE US! I guess we're not really nobodies after all.

The truth is, NOBODY is a nobody. God loves ALL of us. That's why God sent this special baby into the world. Jesus was a gift to every man, woman, and child—the most precious gift God has ever given.

Have *you* ever felt like a nobody? If you have, remember Jesus was born for YOU. And Jesus wants to be friends with you. In fact, you can talk to Jesus right now. Just pray, and he will hear you. He was born to love you!

❧ SHEPHERDS ❧

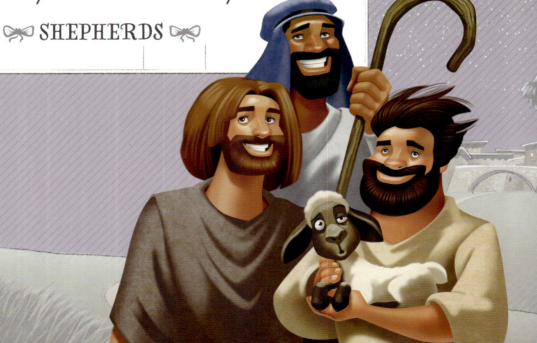

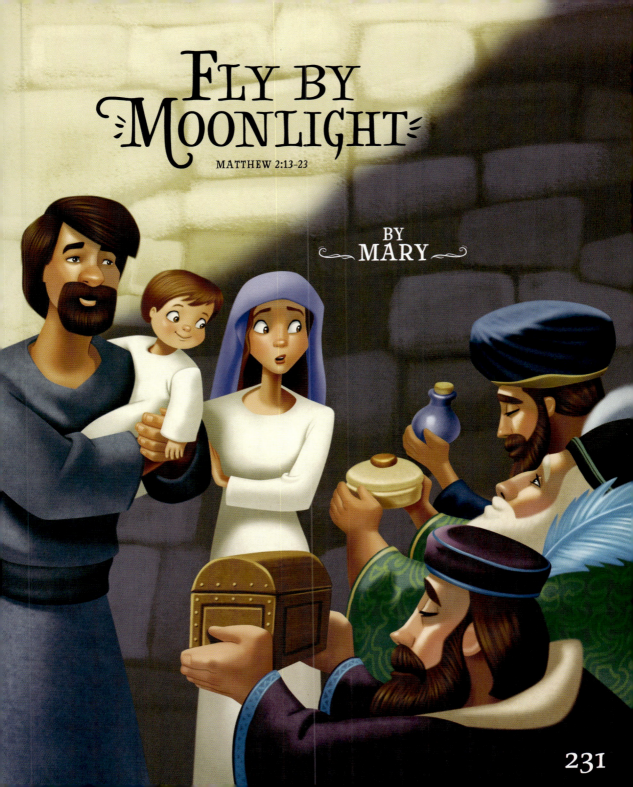

FLY BY MOONLIGHT

MATTHEW 2:13-23

BY MARY

BEING a mom has been one surprise after another. It all started when God chose *me* to be the mother of the most important baby in the whole world. God wanted ME to be Jesus' mom. Can you believe it? I was surprised. No, I was shocked!

And Joseph, the man I was engaged to, was shocked, too. He wasn't even sure he should still marry me. But God told him that everything was all right—this baby was from God!

When it was almost time for our baby to be born, Joseph and I had to go on a long trip. We walked on a dirt road for miles and miles. When we finally got to Bethlehem, we couldn't find a place to stay, so I had my sweet baby in a dirty, smelly manger. No bed—just an old wooden box with hay. But none of that mattered when I looked down at his face. He was perfect!

I loved taking care of little Jesus. But soon, life got even more surprising.

Some wise men from other lands came to our house and gave fancy gifts to Jesus—gold, frankincense, and myrrh. I thought that was unusual, but Jesus wasn't your usual kid.

And then came another surprise—and this one was scary. Jesus' life was in danger! King Herod had heard a new king of the Jews had been born. And Herod wanted that child dead. He even sent out soldiers to kill every boy under the age of two. He wanted to kill Jesus!

I'd do anything to save my little boy. And so would God.

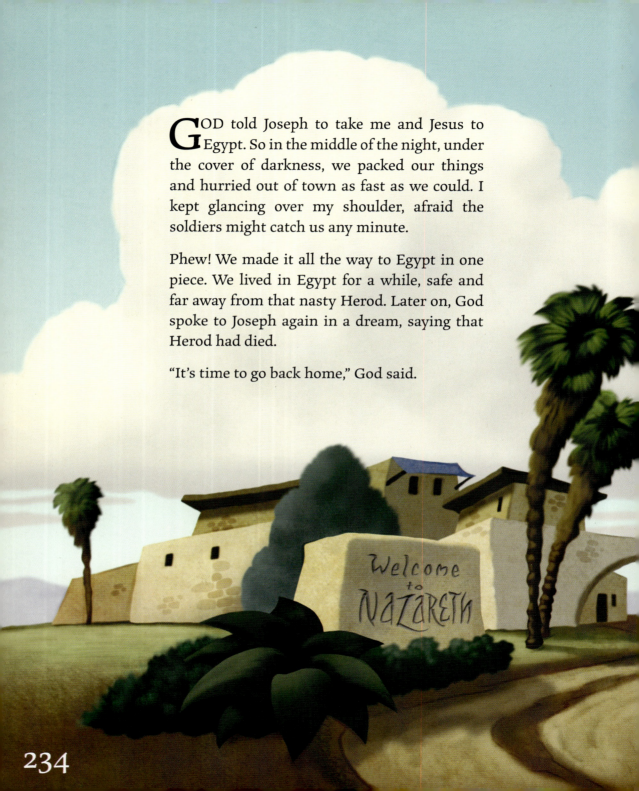

GOD told Joseph to take me and Jesus to Egypt. So in the middle of the night, under the cover of darkness, we packed our things and hurried out of town as fast as we could. I kept glancing over my shoulder, afraid the soldiers might catch us any minute.

Phew! We made it all the way to Egypt in one piece. We lived in Egypt for a while, safe and far away from that nasty Herod. Later on, God spoke to Joseph again in a dream, saying that Herod had died.

"It's time to go back home," God said.

Welcome to NAZARETH

Joseph took Jesus and me back to Israel. But instead of returning to Bethlehem, we made a new home in a town called Nazareth. We thought it'd be a good place to raise our family.

God has always watched out for us. And God wanted us to be safe.

My life has been a whirlwind so far. But I wouldn't trade it for anything. I love being Jesus' mom. And I know God has something special in store for him—something so amazing it will be the biggest surprise of all time.

You know, the world can be really dangerous sometimes. In my case, it was a matter of life and death. As a mother, I'll do anything to protect my child.

Thankfully, God will, too—no matter what happens. Fleeing to Egypt in the dark of night wasn't exactly what we'd been planning. But we were safe, which is what God wanted us to be.

God wants to keep you safe, too.

Who keeps _you_ safe? Name some of the people who care about keeping you out of danger. Then thank God for every one of those people who love you enough to watch out for you.

❧MARY❧

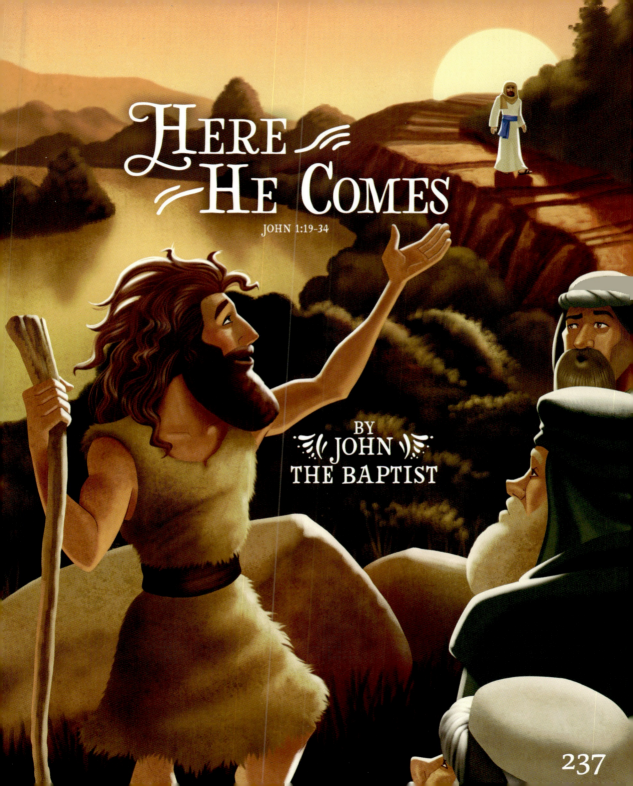

HERE HE COMES

JOHN 1:19-34

BY ⤚ JOHN ⤙
THE BAPTIST

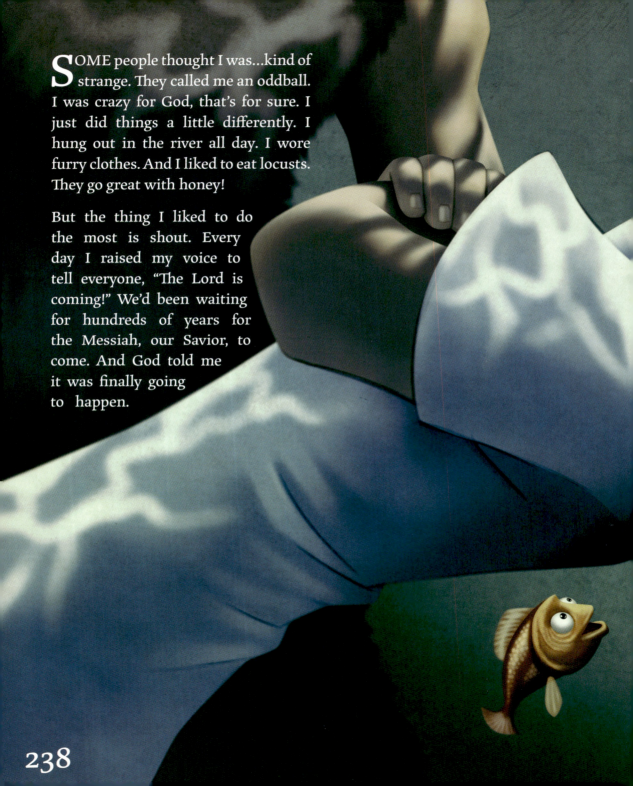

SOME people thought I was...kind of strange. They called me an oddball. I was crazy for God, that's for sure. I just did things a little differently. I hung out in the river all day. I wore furry clothes. And I liked to eat locusts. They go great with honey!

But the thing I liked to do the most is shout. Every day I raised my voice to tell everyone, "The Lord is coming!" We'd been waiting for hundreds of years for the Messiah, our Savior, to come. And God told me it was finally going to happen.

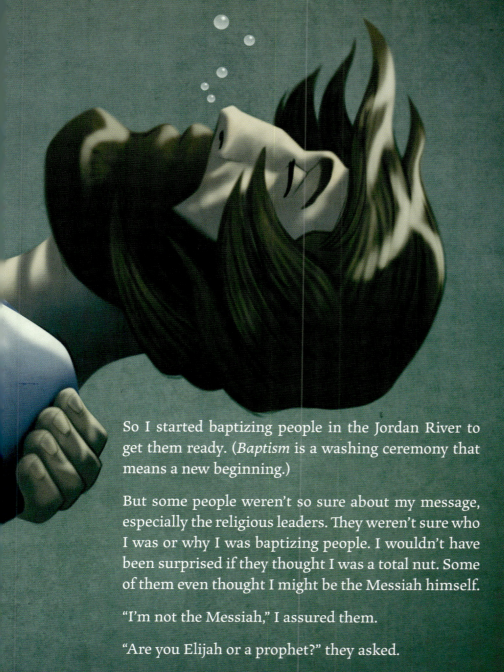

So I started baptizing people in the Jordan River to get them ready. (*Baptism* is a washing ceremony that means a new beginning.)

But some people weren't so sure about my message, especially the religious leaders. They weren't sure who I was or why I was baptizing people. I wouldn't have been surprised if they thought I was a total nut. Some of them even thought I might be the Messiah himself.

"I'm not the Messiah," I assured them.

"Are you Elijah or a prophet?" they asked.

"No," I said. "I'm just a voice shouting in the wilderness, 'The Lord is coming!'"

I know they thought I was strange, but I told them the Messiah was already among us. I said he's far more important than I am. "I'm not even good enough to untie the straps of his sandal!" I said.

The next day I finally saw him: the Messiah. It was JESUS!

"Look! There he is!" I shouted. "The Lamb of God who takes away the sin of the world!"

I knew it was him because I could see the Holy Spirit come down from heaven and rest on him, like a dove. It happened just the way God told me it would.

And God told me something else. I baptized people with ordinary water. But God said Jesus would baptize people with something extraordinary: the Holy Spirit. I can only imagine the amazing things that will happen when Jesus—the Messiah, the Lamb of God—starts doing that!

And I wasn't crazy!

It was an exciting time for us Jews. (Even the odd ones like me.) For hundreds of years we'd been waiting for the Messiah to come, sent from God to save his people once and for all.

And now he had come!

God came to be with us through his Son, Jesus. And Jesus would finally make it possible for us—you and me—to be friends with God.

Did you know *you* can be forever friends with God? God already wants you to be his friend. So do you want to be his friend, too? Let him know; he's crazy about you!

❧ JOHN THE BAPTIST ❧

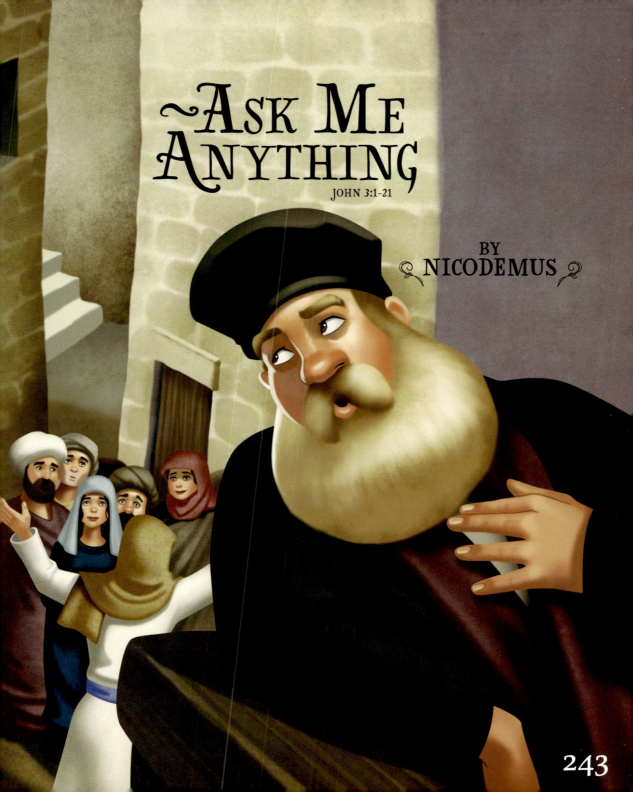

Ask Me Anything

JOHN 3:1-21

BY NICODEMUS

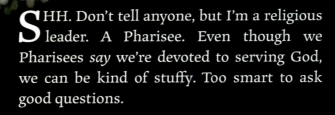

SHH. Don't tell anyone, but I'm a religious leader. A Pharisee. Even though we Pharisees *say* we're devoted to serving God, we can be kind of stuffy. Too smart to ask good questions.

But not me. I'm a curious guy! My friends think I ask too many questions. Like, "Why do bad things happen to good people?" and "What's the meaning of life?"

I was especially curious about Jesus, and I had some BIG questions for him, too. I'd heard about the amazing things he'd done, and I knew that God had sent him to teach us. But Jesus said some strange things I didn't understand.

So one night after dark, I had an idea. I didn't want anyone to catch me talking to Jesus, so I snuck out to find him.

"What do you mean when you say we have to be 'born again' to be in God's kingdom?" I asked Jesus. I didn't get it. "I know it's impossible for a man to go back into his mother's womb."

"I'm talking about your spiritual life," Jesus told me. "Only God's Spirit can give you a spiritual birth."

"That still doesn't make much sense," I said, shaking my head.

"God's Spirit is like the wind. You can't tell where the wind is coming from or where it's going. But that doesn't mean it's not happening," said Jesus.

Huh? I wondered.

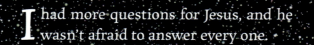

I had more questions for Jesus, and he wasn't afraid to answer every one.

"I'm confused. You're teaching things I've never heard before. You don't make sense to me," I said.

And you know what? Jesus didn't get angry. He was patient with me. "I can tell you what I've seen with my own eyes, yet you still won't believe me. If you can't even believe simple things like that, how are you going to believe me when I tell you about things you can't see, like things of God?"

I wanted to get it. I really did. "Explain it to me one more time."

Then Jesus looked me in the eye and said, "It all comes down to this: God loved the world so much that he sent his Son to save it. If people believe that, they'll live forever. God's Son isn't here to judge the world; he came to set it free."

Wow. Those were the best answers I'd ever heard.

247

He's a smart guy, that Jesus. Way smarter than me, if I'm being honest about it. He talks about God in fresh, new ways. Ways I've never even thought about.

I was confused because I was an old teacher, stuck in my old ways. Jesus talked about God's love like it was something real, like I could have a close friendship with God. We Pharisees never thought about it that way before. It sounded strange.

I hope it doesn't sound strange to you. Jesus knew what he was talking about. And a whole lot of people believed him. And you know what? They all seemed happier and more at peace. That's something I want, too.

Have *you* ever had trouble understanding something? It's always a good idea to talk to someone else when we're confused. Don't be afraid to ask questions. Questions are awesome! Ask your parent or another grown-up you trust a question you've been wondering about.

NICODEMUS

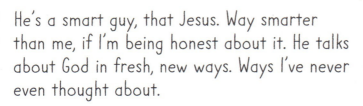

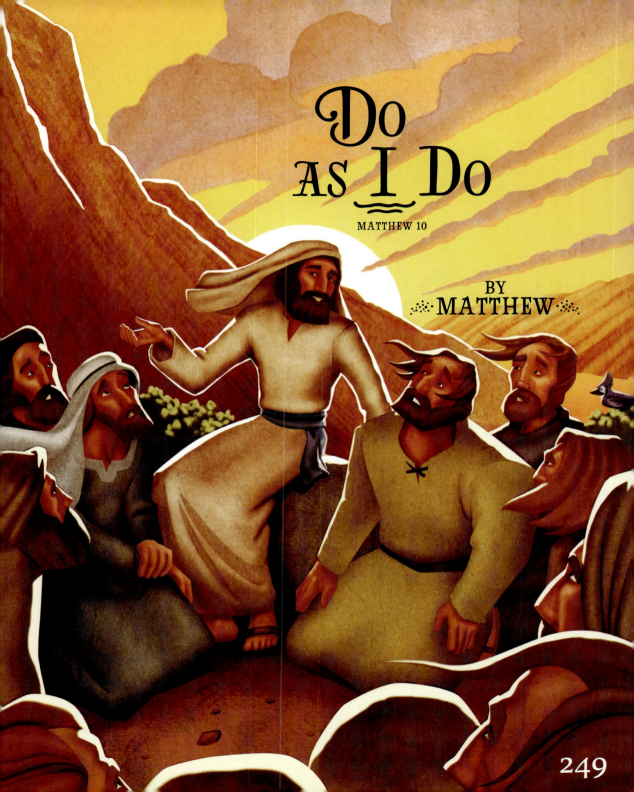

Do As I Do

Matthew 10

By ❖ Matthew ❖

I love our team. There are twelve of us: Peter, Andrew, James and John (the brothers), Philip, Bartholomew, Thomas, James, Thaddaeus, Simon (the zealot), Judas Iscariot, and me, Matthew. We're Jesus' go-to crew, his disciples. Yay, team!

We'd been following Jesus around for quite a while now, and we'd seen him do things that made us say "WOW"—things like healing terrible diseases, making blind people see, bringing dead people back to life, helping crippled people walk—all kinds of miracles.

But now Jesus wanted us to stop watching and start doing. Jesus asked us—his twelve disciples, his closest friends, his team—to do the same things he did.

Whoa! Now because of Jesus' power, we, too, would perform miracles: even raise the dead! We would be changing people's lives right and left. We'd bring smiles to countless faces. We were going to be both Jesus' all-stars and his cheerleaders.

"The kingdom of heaven is near!" we shouted to anyone who would listen.

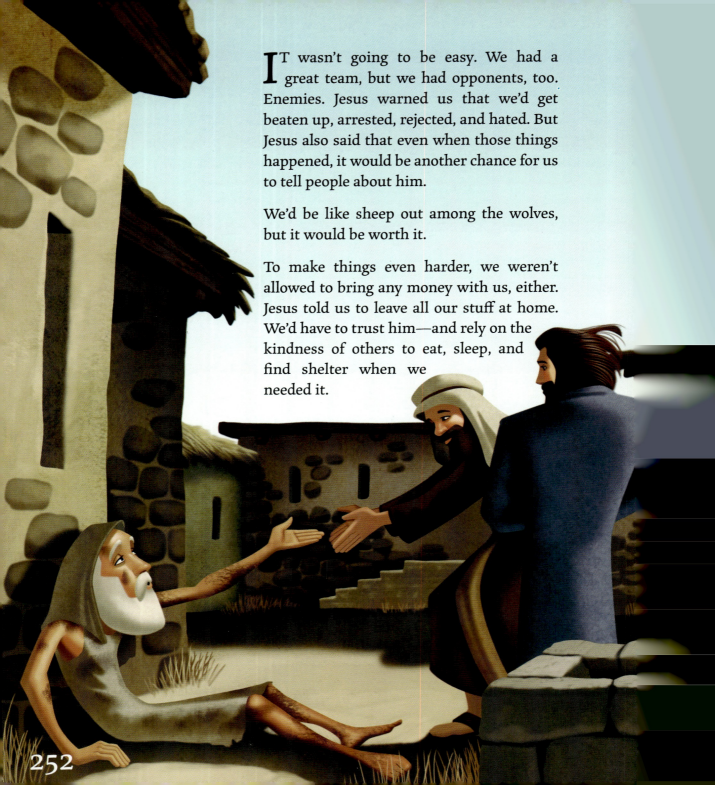

IT wasn't going to be easy. We had a great team, but we had opponents, too. Enemies. Jesus warned us that we'd get beaten up, arrested, rejected, and hated. But Jesus also said that even when those things happened, it would be another chance for us to tell people about him.

We'd be like sheep out among the wolves, but it would be worth it.

To make things even harder, we weren't allowed to bring any money with us, either. Jesus told us to leave all our stuff at home. We'd have to trust him—and rely on the kindness of others to eat, sleep, and find shelter when we needed it.

Sounds hard, right? But we were excited! We weren't worried because we knew God was watching out for us.

Jesus told us something that made a lot of sense: "If God takes care of little birds, then of course God would take care of you, too. God knows every little thing that happens to you. God could even tell you how many hairs are on your head!"

And you know what? God always watched out for us, his team.

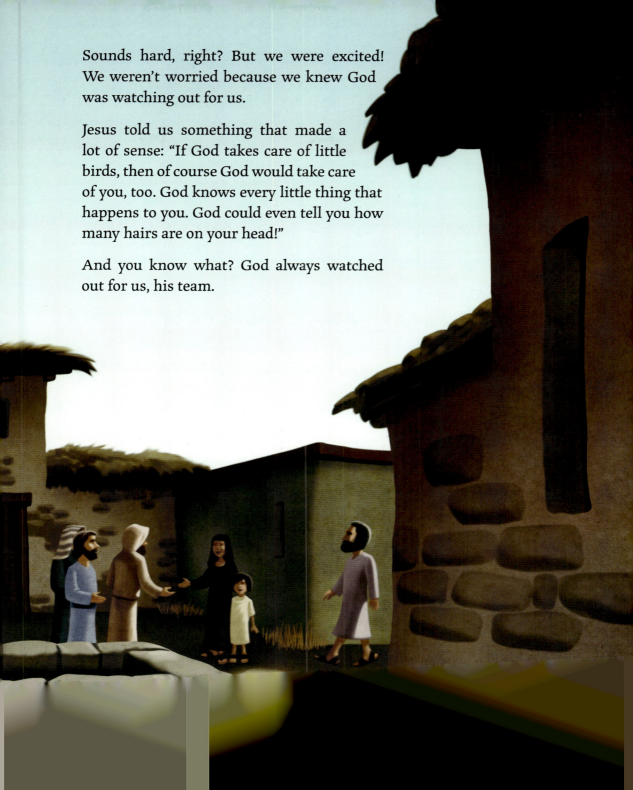

Some people say, "You gave up your whole life for this Jesus guy!" It's true: We gave him everything.

Jesus wants all of us to love him more than anything. That sounds pretty hard, but it doesn't mean we can't love anything else. In fact, the more we love Jesus, the more we're able to love other people.

What about you? Do you want to join our team? You can!

Being on Jesus' team means following him. And there's lots of stuff *you* can do for Jesus. Be generous and kind to others, for one thing. Jesus said when we show love to other people, then we're loving him, too.

◎◎◎ MATTHEW ◎◎◎

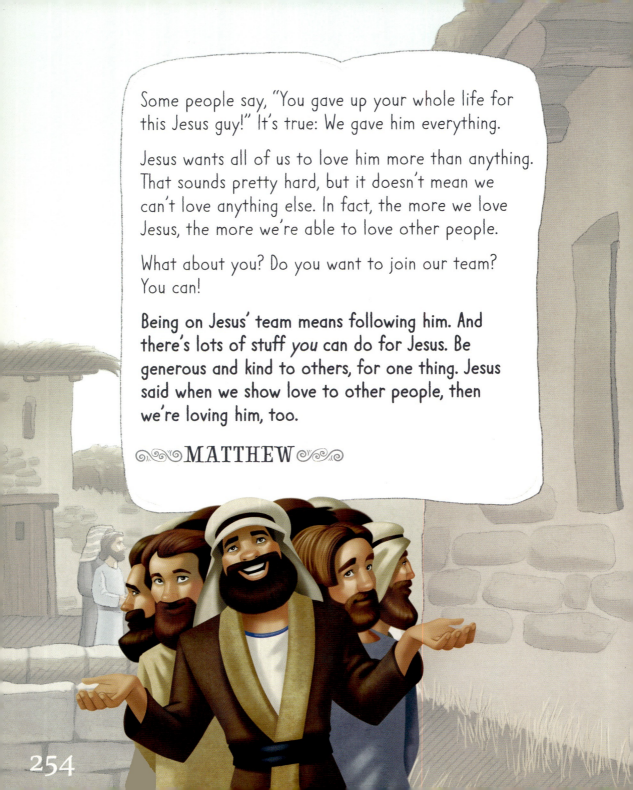

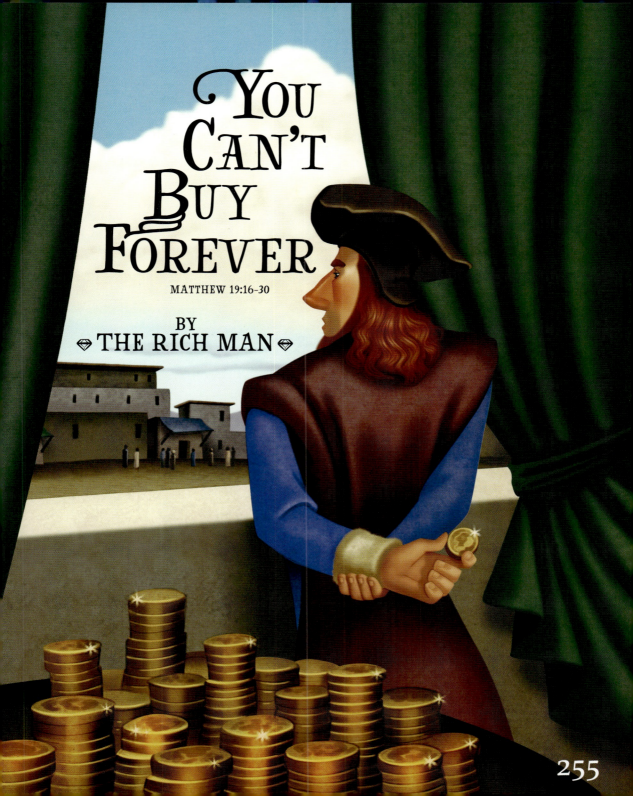

You Can't Buy Forever

MATTHEW 19:16-30

BY

◈ THE RICH MAN ◈

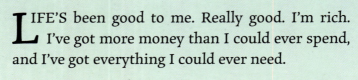

LIFE'S been good to me. Really good. I'm rich. I've got more money than I could ever spend, and I've got everything I could ever need.

But if there's one thing I want more than anything else, it's to live forever. All the money in the world just can't fill this empty feeling I have inside me.

I'd heard about a teacher named Jesus. People were calling him the Son of God. The Messiah. They said he had the answers to everything, including how to live forever.

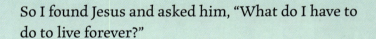

So I found Jesus and asked him, "What do I have to do to live forever?"

"Simple," Jesus said. "Keep God's commandments. Don't murder, don't cheat, don't steal, don't lie, respect your parents, and love other people."

"I've done that! I'm a really good guy. Is there anything else?" I asked.

Jesus folded his arms and said, "If you're *really* serious, sell everything you own and give all the money to poor people. Then come and follow me."

WHAT?! Sell everything I own? Give all my money away? And follow Jesus? Follow him *where*?

Hmm.

That was too much to ask. There's no way I could walk away from my comfortable life. I had it made for now.

So I walked away from Jesus instead.

As I headed in the other direction, I overheard Jesus talking to his disciples.

"It is very, very hard for rich people to get into God's kingdom. It's like trying to put a camel through the eye of a needle!" Jesus said. *Well, that's impossible,* I thought.

"Then how can people be saved?" one of his disciples asked.

"It's impossible for people to do on their own. But with God, ANYTHING can happen," Jesus said. "And God will be very generous to those who've given up everything for him. Those who think they're really important now are going to end up at the bottom of the pile."

Ouch. Jesus didn't say what I wanted to hear. I was really hoping there was some way I could buy my way into heaven. I guess there's not.

I can't help wondering: What do people need to do to earn their way into heaven?

Jesus said it was impossible. We can't do it by ourselves. We can't buy it. We can't earn it.

All we have to do is believe it. Then God makes it possible.

It's God's gift to us.

Why do you think we want to buy our way into heaven or do enough good things to get into heaven? It's amazing that it's really a gift, made possible only by Jesus himself.

ꙮ THE RICH MAN ꙮ

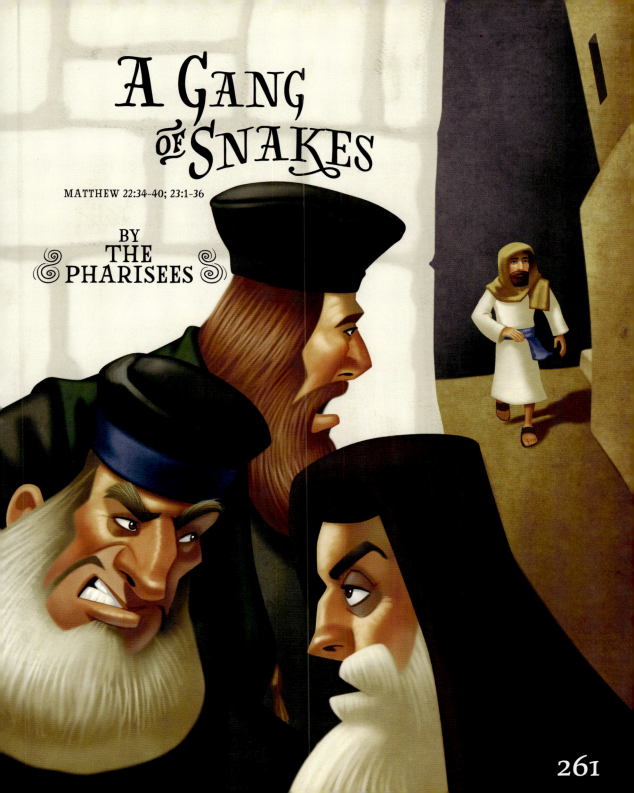

A GANG OF SNAKES

MATTHEW 22:34-40; 23:1-36

BY THE PHARISEES

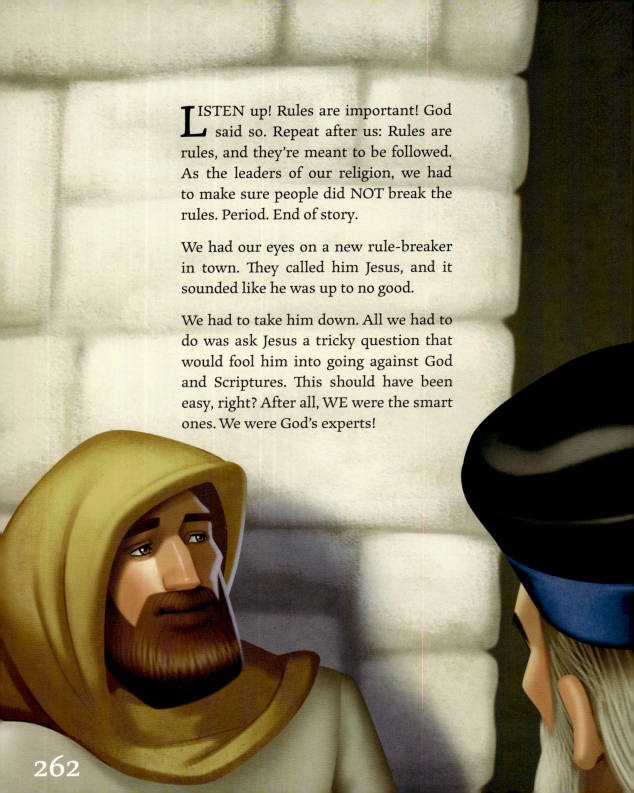

LISTEN up! Rules are important! God said so. Repeat after us: Rules are rules, and they're meant to be followed. As the leaders of our religion, we had to make sure people did NOT break the rules. Period. End of story.

We had our eyes on a new rule-breaker in town. They called him Jesus, and it sounded like he was up to no good.

We had to take him down. All we had to do was ask Jesus a tricky question that would fool him into going against God and Scriptures. This should have been easy, right? After all, WE were the smart ones. We were God's experts!

When we saw Jesus, we raised our chins, cleared our throats, and asked him, "What is the most important commandment?" We smiled to ourselves because we knew there was no way he could give us the right answer.

But Jesus didn't even hesitate. "Love God with everything you have. But there's a second commandment that's just as important. Love other people as much as you love yourself. If you obey these two things, all the other rules will make sense."

RATS! We couldn't argue with that. We frowned, folded our arms, and started walking away. But then Jesus began talking to the crowd of people around us.

"These Pharisees are good at teaching the law. You should listen to them," Jesus started to say.

At first we liked where Jesus was going with this. Maybe he wasn't so bad after all. But then he laid into us—big time.

"But DON'T do what the Pharisees do! All they care about is the rules and how they look. They don't care about you. All they do is make it harder for you to grow closer to God. They love the attention, but they don't love you!" Jesus shouted.

He went on and on and on. Jesus called us fools and fakes and snakes! He said we were blind! He even said we were no better than tombs—something that looks nice on the outside but is full of death on the inside.

We didn't like Jesus. Not one bit! We needed to do something about that troublemaker.

But first we had more rules to enforce.

(By the way, don't these robes look good? Only the finest fabrics, of course. We think they make us look super-important.)

Fakes?! Is that what Jesus thinks we are? We teach the RULES, for goodness' sake! There's nothing fake about the rules. God made them, after all. We're just trying to make them...better. If a rule is really hard to follow, it must be a good rule!

Clearly Jesus doesn't think that way. He goes on and on about LOVING people. That's all well and good...until someone starts breaking the rules again.

Hmmph.

What would *you* do? Ask one of your friends these two questions: How does it make you feel when all someone cares about is making everyone follow the rules? And how does it make you feel when someone is kind to you?

THE PHARISEES

The Best for the Best

JOHN 12:1–8

BY MARY

I loved Jesus so much. Especially because I didn't feel very lovable. But *he loves me!*

I wanted everyone to know he's the Messiah. He's come to save us and set us free from our sins. That meant the world to me! He heals people and performs miracles we've never seen before!

I really wanted to do something to honor him. He's the Son of God, after all. He deserves the best I can give him.

The best I had was a fancy jar of perfume. It was very, very expensive: worth as much money as you could earn in a whole year. Jesus has done so much for me. How could I give him anything less?

Jesus was eating dinner at Simon's house with some friends, so I rushed over to give Jesus my gift.

I went straight to Jesus and dropped to my knees. I took my perfume and poured it all over his feet, and then wiped it with my long hair.

Jesus' friends looked shocked.

"How could you let her do that!" one of them said to Jesus, waving his hands in the air.

"What a waste!" another one groaned.

"We could have sold that perfume and given the money to the poor!" a third one said, his face turning red.

Jesus shook his head. "Leave her alone. She's doing something good. You can feed poor people for the rest of your lives, but I'm not going to be around much longer."

Then Jesus looked in my eyes and smiled. "What you've done will be remembered forever," he told me.

I would do it again in a heartbeat.

I gave Jesus the most valuable thing I had. But it wasn't what you think it is; it wasn't the perfume.

It was *me*.

That's what Jesus wants more than anything. He wants us. WE are the best gift we could ever give to Jesus.

What's the most valuable thing *you* own? How would it feel to give that thing to someone else? That's kind of what it feels like to give ourselves to Jesus.

One thing I know for sure: Jesus doesn't want our things. He wants our hearts.

MARY

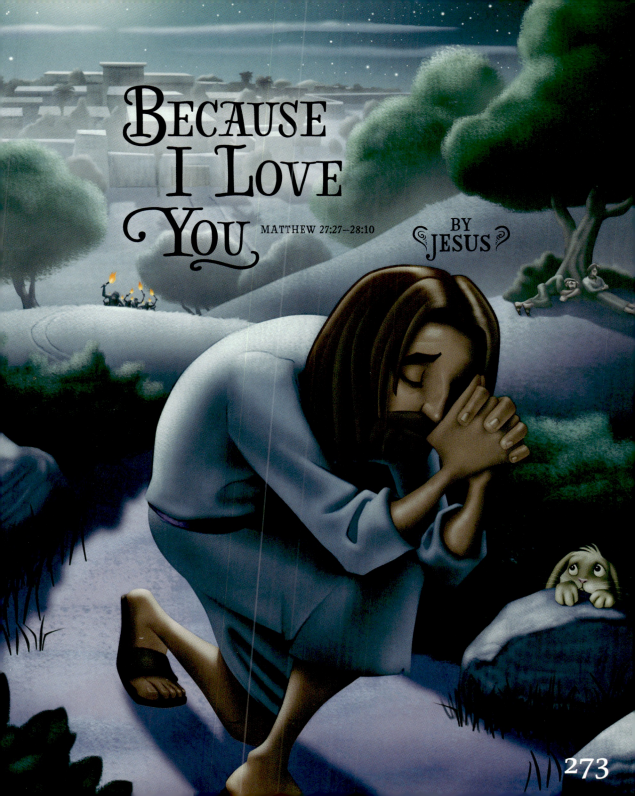

Because I Love You

MATTHEW 27:27—28:10

BY JESUS

I'M going to tell you the most important story ever told. It won't be easy for you to hear. But I promise you this: It has the happiest ending in the history of happy endings.

It started when the Roman soldiers arrested me while I was praying. One of my dearest friends had betrayed me to them, and all for a little bit of money. That hurt.

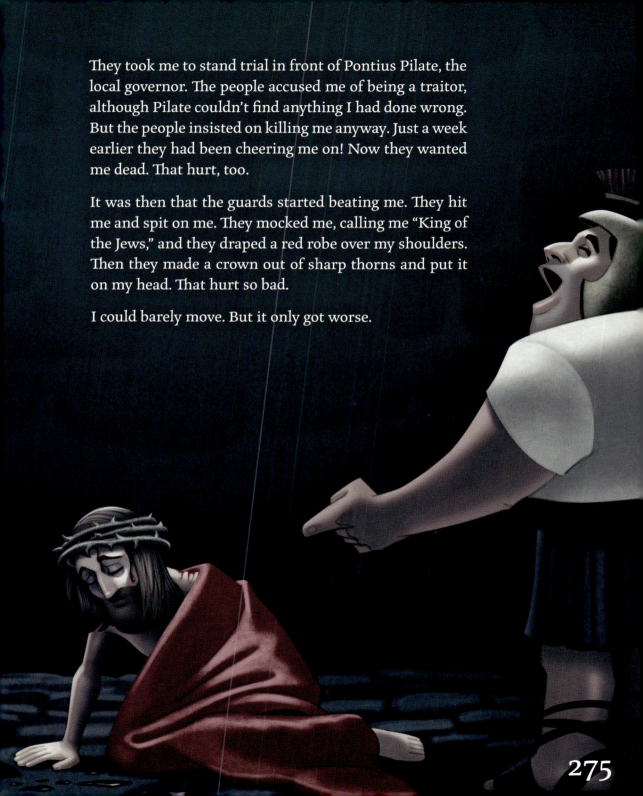

They took me to stand trial in front of Pontius Pilate, the local governor. The people accused me of being a traitor, although Pilate couldn't find anything I had done wrong. But the people insisted on killing me anyway. Just a week earlier they had been cheering me on! Now they wanted me dead. That hurt, too.

It was then that the guards started beating me. They hit me and spit on me. They mocked me, calling me "King of the Jews," and they draped a red robe over my shoulders. Then they made a crown out of sharp thorns and put it on my head. That hurt so bad.

I could barely move. But it only got worse.

275

THE guards made a big cross out of wooden beams. Even though I had no strength left, they made me carry that cross, with people along the road yelling at me. It was so heavy. Every step was torture. When I finally couldn't go any farther, they made another man carry that heavy cross for me.

They marched me up a hill to a creepy area they called the Place of the Skull. The pain was unbearable. I could barely catch my breath. The soldiers tried to give me a bitter drink to ease the pain, but I wouldn't take a sip. I needed to endure every jolt, every stab, every sting. And there were so many.

I had nothing left.

Still, they kept mocking me.

"If you're the Son of God, why don't you save yourself?" they shouted.

But they didn't know. They didn't understand that God wanted me to go through with this. They didn't know this was God's plan. Worst of all, they didn't realize how much I loved them. Every tear and every drop of blood was for *them*.

IT was almost the end. The sky turned black. Every breath was a struggle. I'd never felt more alone in my life.

I hung my head. I couldn't take another breath.

The moment I died, things got scary. The ground shook. Rocks split apart. People wept. The curtain in the Temple sanctuary split in half. Tombs opened up, and dead people began to come back to life.

That terrified the soldiers. They realized in an instant what they had done: They had killed me, God's Son.

Later, a rich man named Joseph took my body and wrapped it in cloths. Then he buried me in a tomb carved out of the rocks and rolled a big stone across the entrance.

Yet my killers were nervous. They'd heard me talk about coming back from the dead. They thought my followers might come to steal my body and claim I wasn't dead anymore. So they placed guards there to make sure nothing happened.

But something *did* happen.

279

THREE days later everything changed.

As soon as the sun cracked the morning sky, an earthquake rattled the tomb as one of God's radiant angels swept down and rolled the stone away. Then he hopped up and sat on it!

The guards were so scared they passed out.

Just then Mary Magdalene and my other friend named Mary came to visit the tomb. But when they saw the angel, their jaws dropped.

"Don't be afraid," said the angel. "Jesus isn't here anymore. He's alive again! Hurry and go tell his followers!"

Mary Magdalene and Mary took one glance at the empty tomb and started running fast! They were frightened and excited and shocked and thrilled all at the same time. And when they saw me standing in the middle of the road, they ran even faster.

"YOU'RE ALIVE!" they cried.

And I would stay alive this time.

Forever.

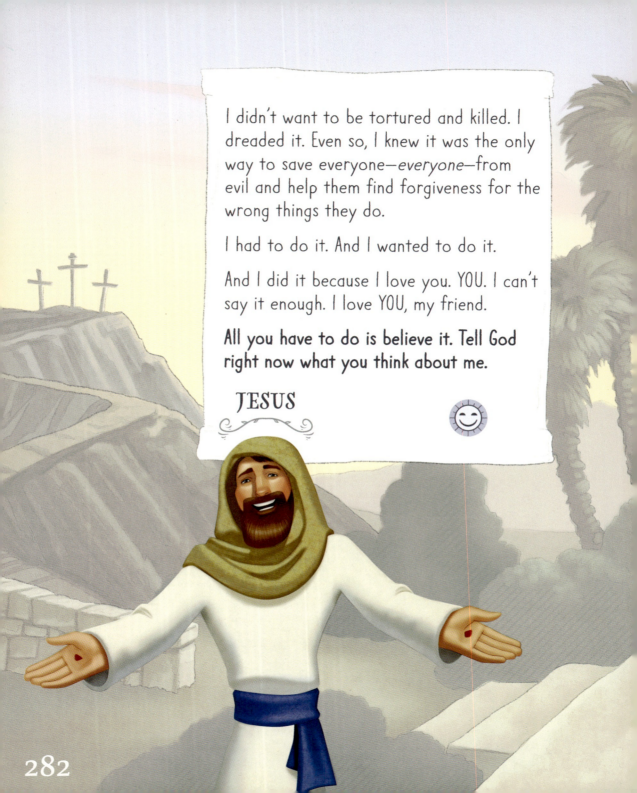

I didn't want to be tortured and killed. I dreaded it. Even so, I knew it was the only way to save everyone—*everyone*—from evil and help them find forgiveness for the wrong things they do.

I had to do it. And I wanted to do it.

And I did it because I love you. YOU. I can't say it enough. I love YOU, my friend.

All you have to do is believe it. Tell God right now what you think about me.

JESUS

282

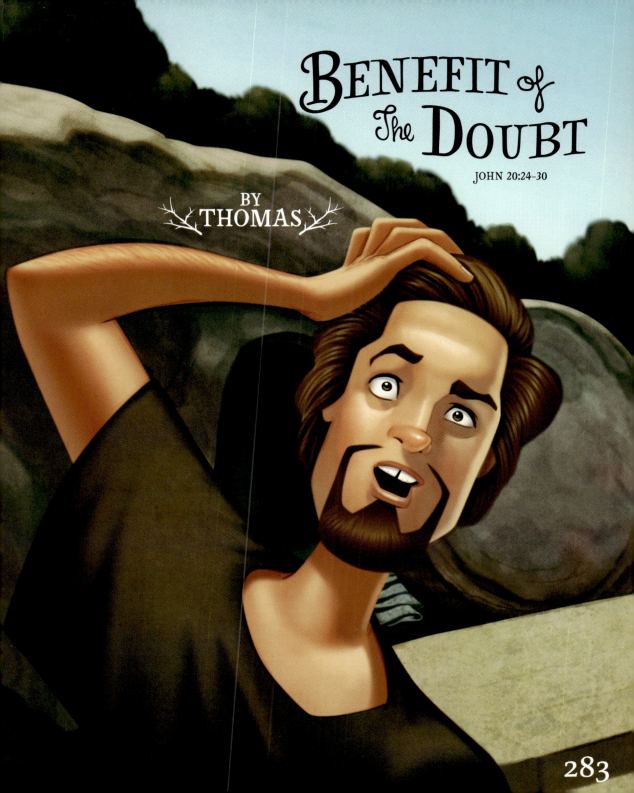

Benefit of the Doubt

JOHN 20:24-30

BY THOMAS

I saw Jesus die with my own eyes.

The other disciples told me they had seen Jesus alive. Alive? Really?! That's impossible. Sure, Jesus may have raised a few other folks from the dead, but raise *himself*? Doubtful.

I needed evidence.

Look, I was raised a fisherman. Unless I saw an actual fish in my net, I knew I wouldn't be taking anything home for dinner.

284

And I knew what I'd already seen. I could hardly bear to see the Roman soldiers hammering spikes into Jesus' hands and feet. I saw them spear him in the side with a sword. I saw Jesus die with my own eyes. I even watched a friend carry his lifeless body into the tomb.

Plus, I didn't want to get my hopes up. I loved Jesus with all my heart. Watching him die was the hardest thing I've ever done. I didn't want to go through that pain again.

Unless I could put my very own fingers into the wounds in Jesus' hands and feet, I wouldn't believe it. I wanted proof.

ABOUT a week later the disciples invited me over for dinner. We locked the doors because we were still afraid the Romans might be looking for us, Jesus' followers.

Then the strangest thing happened.

Suddenly there was another person in the room. He hadn't opened the door or crawled through a window. He was just...*there*.

"He looks a lot like Jesus," I whispered.

Jesus smiled and said, "Peace, friends."

Then he walked straight up to me and held out his hands. "Here's your proof, Thomas. Go ahead, touch my wounds. They're as real as you are."

My hands were shaking as I slowly reached out. I felt the rough skin where the spikes had cut through his hands. I touched the mark in his side where he'd been stabbed.

"Jesus!" I cried. "It's really YOU!"

Jesus didn't reject me because I had some doubts. People like me need to see things to believe them. Jesus knew that. And he loved me anyway.

I spent the rest of my life believing Jesus and serving him.

Jesus wasn't afraid of my doubts, and he's not afraid of yours, either. Yet he also said that people who believe in him—even though they can't see him—are truly blessed. You've never seen him in person, but Jesus wants you to believe in him all the same. And you'll be blessed for it!

Even though you won't see Jesus walking down your street, he is real and at work all around you. Even though you can't see Jesus' physical body today, you can see evidence of him all around, like when someone is kind to a stranger or gives food to a poor person. What do *you* see?

THOMAS

That's the Spirit!

ACTS 2

BY EARLY CHRISTIANS

YOU know that feeling you get right before you're about to go to your own birthday party? That's how we felt in those first few days when Jesus' church was just getting started.

So much had already happened since Jesus died. Not only did Jesus come back to life, but he also performed more miracles, healed the sick, and spent as much time with us as he could. What a wonderful forty days!

What in the world might happen next?

During a meal with us, Jesus told us to stay in Jerusalem until God sent us a gift: the Holy Spirit. What was *that* going to be like? After Jesus floated up into heaven (which was quite a sight, let me tell you), all his followers started getting together whenever we could.

One morning, more than a week after Jesus went away, we were together in a room when all of a sudden we heard a LOUD roaring sound, like some kind of hurricane hit us. Then, just like that, each one of us had flames dancing on the tops of our heads. Incredible!

We felt different. We felt...filled.

We felt empowered.

291

THEN we all started speaking different languages—languages none of us had spoken before—and we could still understand one another. Amazing! In fact, other Jews in Jerusalem were hearing their own languages being spoken by us. More amazing!

People in the city wondered what in the world was going on. They watched us, thunderstruck.

"How is this possible?" they wondered.

"What does it all mean?" they asked.

Some of them shrugged their shoulders and said, "They're all just drunk!"

But Peter stood up and explained what was going on.

"What you're seeing has never happened before," Peter said. "Jesus, the Messiah himself, was killed and came back from the dead to save us all from the bad things we do. Now that Jesus is in heaven, God has given US his Holy Spirit. And now we're going to do amazing things for God!"

We're so excited! Let's get to it!

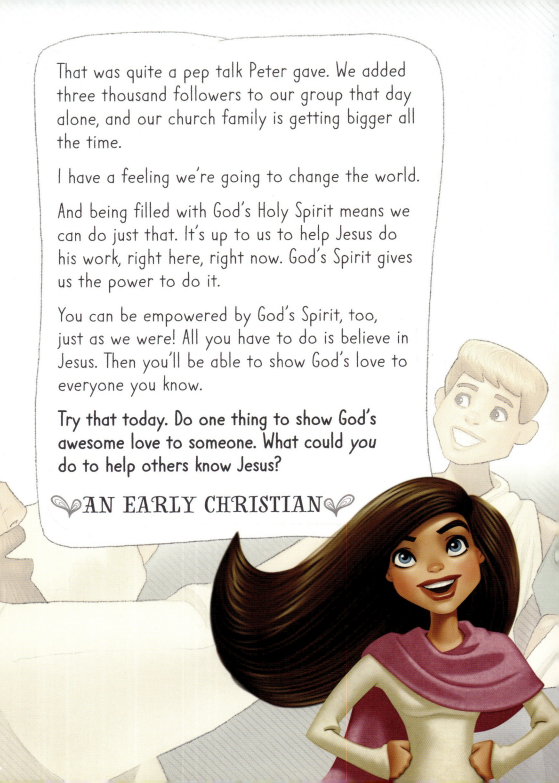

That was quite a pep talk Peter gave. We added three thousand followers to our group that day alone, and our church family is getting bigger all the time.

I have a feeling we're going to change the world.

And being filled with God's Holy Spirit means we can do just that. It's up to us to help Jesus do his work, right here, right now. God's Spirit gives us the power to do it.

You can be empowered by God's Spirit, too, just as we were! All you have to do is believe in Jesus. Then you'll be able to show God's love to everyone you know.

Try that today. Do one thing to show God's awesome love to someone. What could *you* do to help others know Jesus?

AN EARLY CHRISTIAN

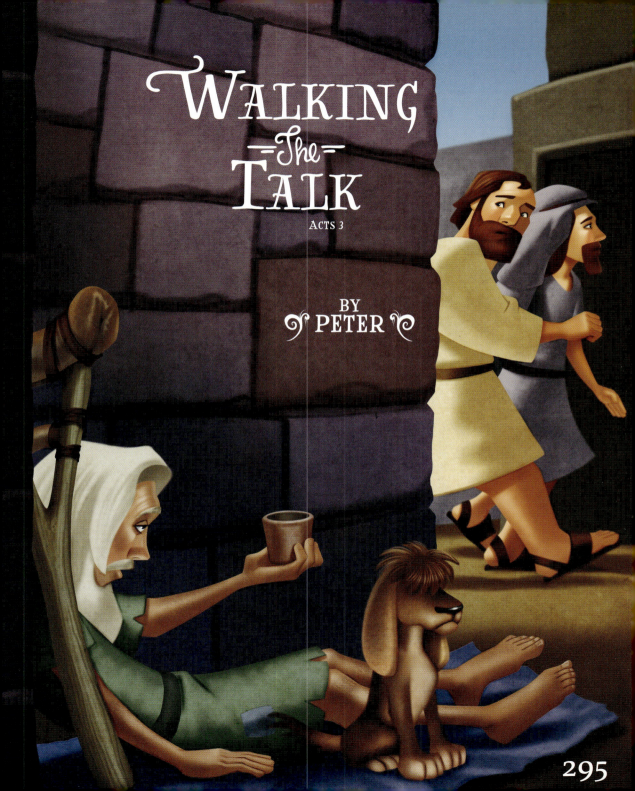

Walking the Talk

Acts 3

By Peter

PEOPLE who know me say I can be rather, uh, bold. Yes, BOLD! I have the guts to do daring things, like that time John and I were walking to the Temple to pray.

It was a normal day: same busy streets, same noisy crowd, same old everything. But this one guy caught my attention. He was crippled, begging for coins like he always did. His skinny legs were weak and twisted, just like they'd been since the day he was born.

"Excuse me!" he called out. "Can you give me some money? Anything? Please!"

I stopped and stared at him for a moment. He stared back, his eyes pleading with us. I could feel God's love for this man flowing through me. I remembered when Jesus said we would be able to perform miracles just like he did.

Now was my chance to do something bold.

"I don't have any money. But I can give you something way better," I said. Next I got bold, because of Jesus. I reached out my hand and spoke. "In the name of Jesus, get up and walk!"

He grabbed my hand and held it tight. Then, for the first time in his life, he jumped up. The man landed on his feet and then took a step. And then another. Next thing we knew he was leaping around like an overjoyed puppy!

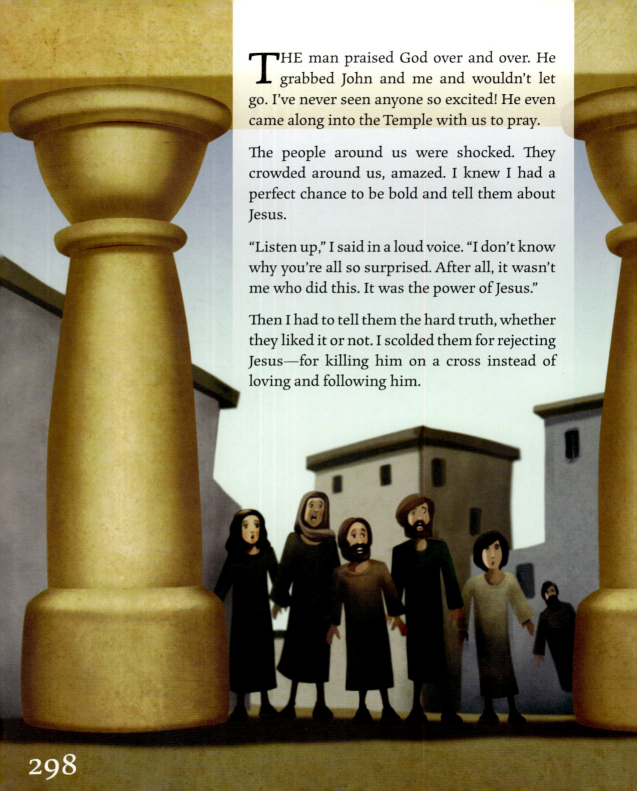

THE man praised God over and over. He grabbed John and me and wouldn't let go. I've never seen anyone so excited! He even came along into the Temple with us to pray.

The people around us were shocked. They crowded around us, amazed. I knew I had a perfect chance to be bold and tell them about Jesus.

"Listen up," I said in a loud voice. "I don't know why you're all so surprised. After all, it wasn't me who did this. It was the power of Jesus."

Then I had to tell them the hard truth, whether they liked it or not. I scolded them for rejecting Jesus—for killing him on a cross instead of loving and following him.

"You didn't really know what you were doing. Plus, Jesus had to die so all the prophecies would come true. But now's your chance to do the right thing! Say you're sorry for the wrong things you've done, and follow Jesus.

"Through faith in the name of Jesus, this man was healed. He walked for the first time in his life. Just think what faith in Jesus can do for *you*!"

I can't even count how many beggars I've seen in my life. I've lost track of the number of sick or hurt people I've walked past over the years. But sometimes all it takes is one person to stand out and make a difference in people's lives.

God gave me compassion for that man. And God knew that healing him would help people understand the power of Jesus.

Now, Jesus didn't come to make everyone perfectly healthy while they're living here on earth. Jesus came to give us a chance to live with him forever, a chance to be perfect with him long after we've left this earth.

Jesus knows what's most important: growing closer to him, just like you would with a best friend. Take some time right now to talk with Jesus in the same way *you* would talk with a friend sitting next to you.

PETER

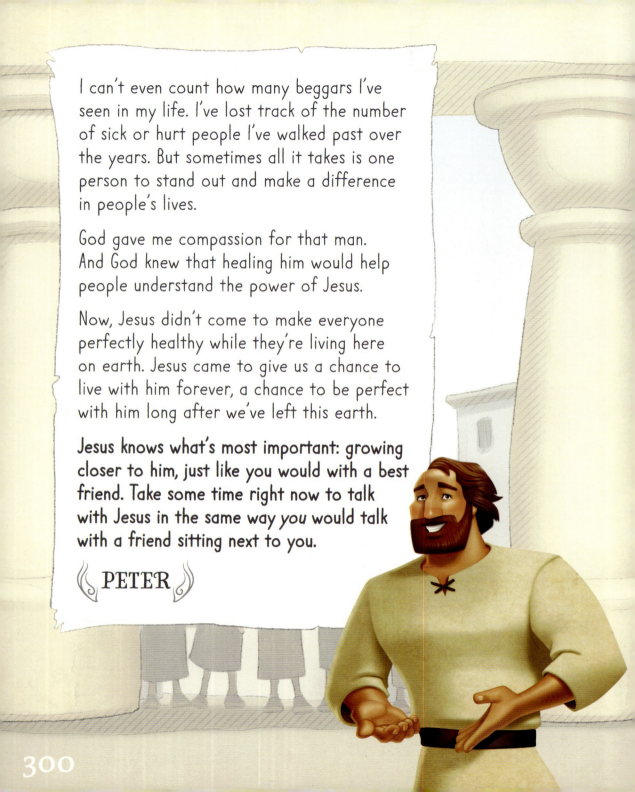

Eyes on Heaven

ACTS 7

BY STEPHEN

I may be dead, but I will always love the people who killed me. Sound strange? Let me explain.

I couldn't blame them. Not really. The priests and religious teachers hated *anyone* who said Jesus was their Messiah. And I wasn't afraid to shout it from the rooftops: "Jesus is MY Messiah!"

They argued with me till they were blue in the face. I tried to tell them how Jesus really came to set us free from the old laws. The truth was on my side, and they lost every argument.

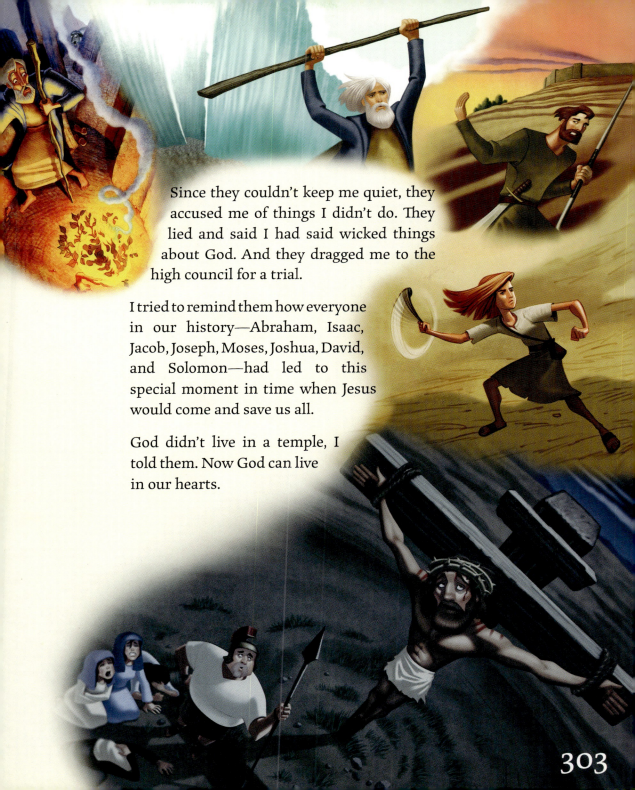

Since they couldn't keep me quiet, they accused me of things I didn't do. They lied and said I had said wicked things about God. And they dragged me to the high council for a trial.

I tried to remind them how everyone in our history—Abraham, Isaac, Jacob, Joseph, Moses, Joshua, David, and Solomon—had led to this special moment in time when Jesus would come and save us all.

God didn't live in a temple, I told them. Now God can live in our hearts.

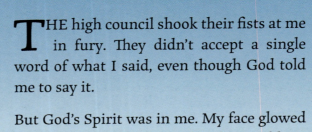

THE high council shook their fists at me in fury. They didn't accept a single word of what I said, even though God told me to say it.

But God's Spirit was in me. My face glowed as bright as an angel's. Suddenly I could see heaven itself, with Jesus standing right next to God. It was a glorious sight!

I tried to tell them more, but they stopped listening. They covered their ears so they couldn't hear me. They shouted as loud as they could. Then they grabbed me by the arms and dragged me out of the city.

Their stones were waiting.

The priests' angry faces twisted with rage as they threw their rocks at me. But I was at peace. Jesus always told us to love our enemies. So I begged God not to hold it against them for hurting me.

Through it all, I kept my gaze on Jesus, knowing that he loved me. Soon I would be with him, and no one would ever hurt me again.

It's not easy to forgive people who hate you. Even I couldn't do that on my own. It was only through the love of Jesus that I could look at the people who wanted me dead and not hate them back.

It might not be too hard to forgive someone who takes your toy and plays with it without asking you first. Yet it's far more difficult to forgive someone who takes your toy and smashes it into pieces.

God wants us to forgive either way. When we forgive others for hurting us, we set ourselves free from bad things—things like anger and hatred.

Is there someone in *your* life who did something to hurt you? Have you stayed mad at that person for a long time? Pray to God that he will give you the strength and love you need to forgive.

✬ STEPHEN ✬

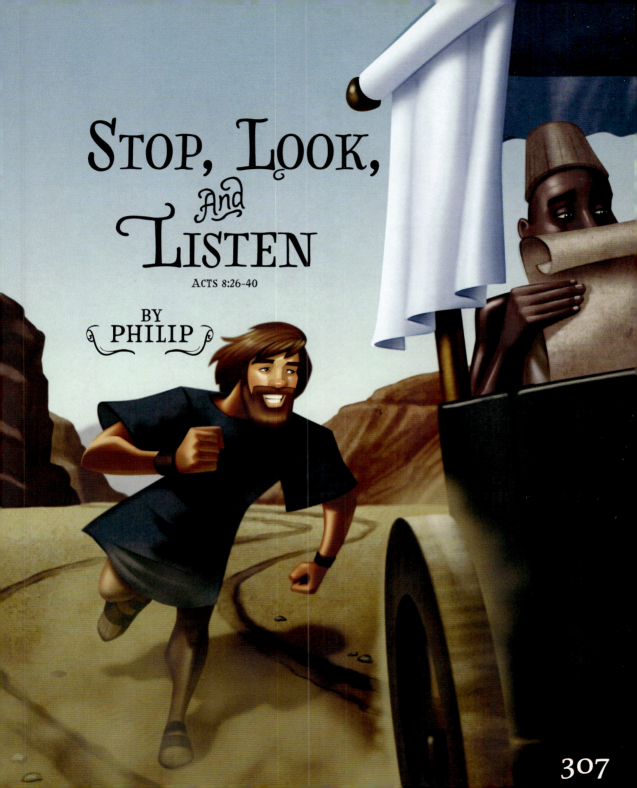

Stop, Look, And Listen

ACTS 8:26-40

BY PHILIP

I'M a doer. A go-getter. And I'm always ready for action. So whenever God's Spirit says go, I go.

Like the time God told me to walk from Jerusalem down to Gaza. It was going to be a long trip, so I got right up, stretched my legs, and started walking. It didn't take long for me to run into someone God wanted me to meet.

He was a man from Ethiopia, a country far away from Israel. He was riding in a fancy carriage, so I figured he must be important. And he was! He turned out to be the Queen of Ethiopia's treasurer.

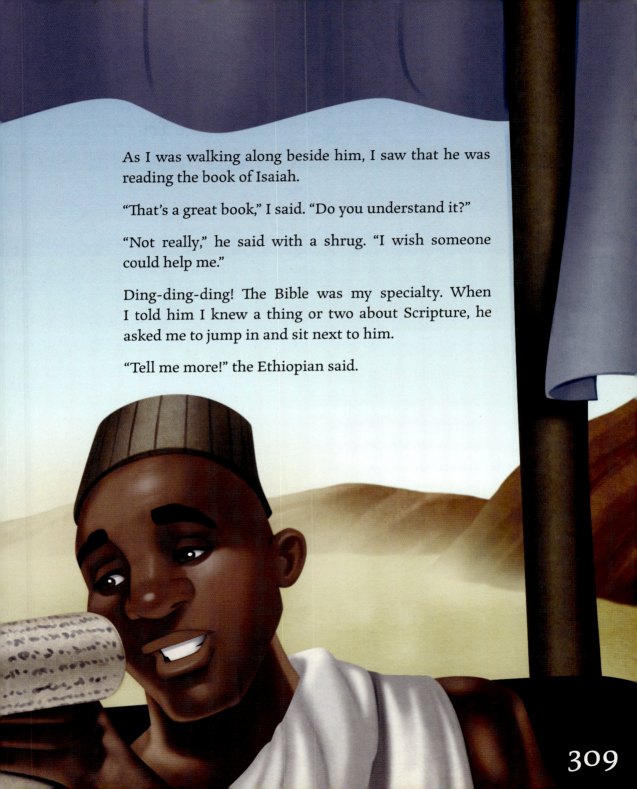

As I was walking along beside him, I saw that he was reading the book of Isaiah.

"That's a great book," I said. "Do you understand it?"

"Not really," he said with a shrug. "I wish someone could help me."

Ding-ding-ding! The Bible was my specialty. When I told him I knew a thing or two about Scripture, he asked me to jump in and sit next to him.

"Tell me more!" the Ethiopian said.

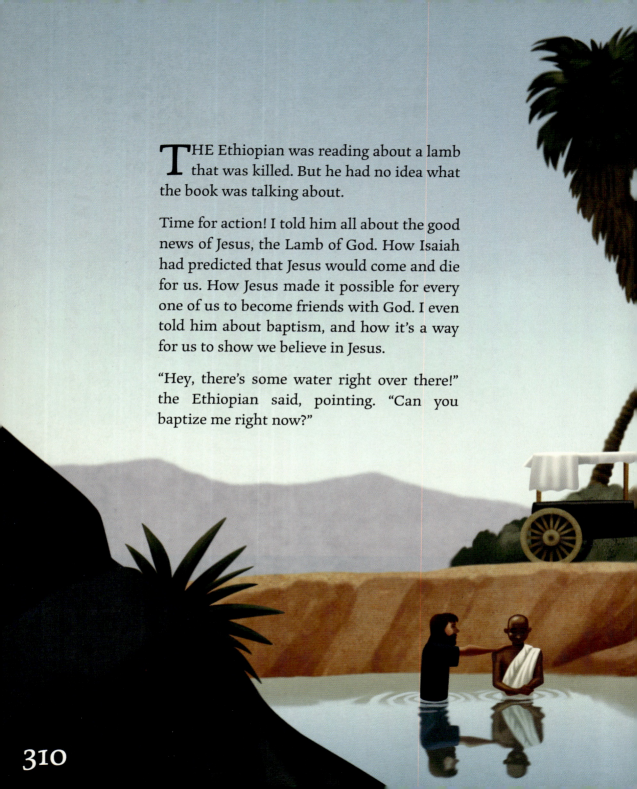

THE Ethiopian was reading about a lamb that was killed. But he had no idea what the book was talking about.

Time for action! I told him all about the good news of Jesus, the Lamb of God. How Isaiah had predicted that Jesus would come and die for us. How Jesus made it possible for every one of us to become friends with God. I even told him about baptism, and how it's a way for us to show we believe in Jesus.

"Hey, there's some water right over there!" the Ethiopian said, pointing. "Can you baptize me right now?"

Like I said, I'm a doer. So of course I said yes. We stopped the carriage and hopped out. We walked into the river together, and I baptized him right on the spot.

Then a strange thing happened.

When the Ethiopian came up out of the water, he must've been shocked because I had disappeared! God's Spirit whisked me away—my whole body and everything—to a whole other town!

(Though I heard the Ethiopian was quite happy anyway. He went on his way rejoicing about his new faith in Jesus.)

I was one of Jesus' twelve disciples, so I know a thing or two about seeing God in action. Sometimes God gives us a little nudge. Other times God sweeps us off our feet!

Both ways are all God's doing. And both ways can lead to wonderful things. God nudged me to take a trip, and I got a chance to share the love of Jesus with someone. Then God performed a miracle, and it was a story I'll never forget.

God's Spirit does that for *you*, too. Have you ever felt a poke in the back of your mind telling you to do something good for someone? That could be God's Spirit. Or have you had a thought that reminds you of someone you could pray for? That's God's Spirit, too.

Be on the lookout for God. Try paying attention for the rest of the day to any nudge you feel to do something kind for a friend.

PHILIP

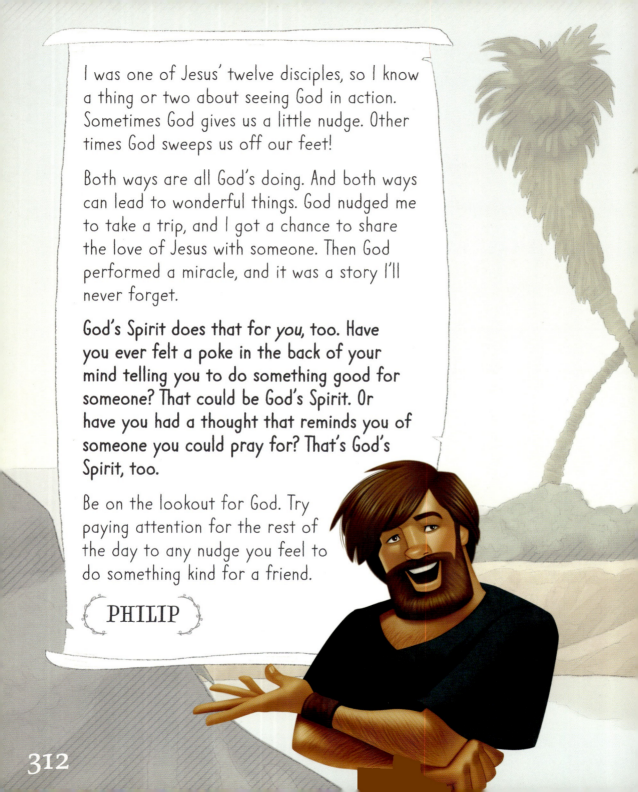

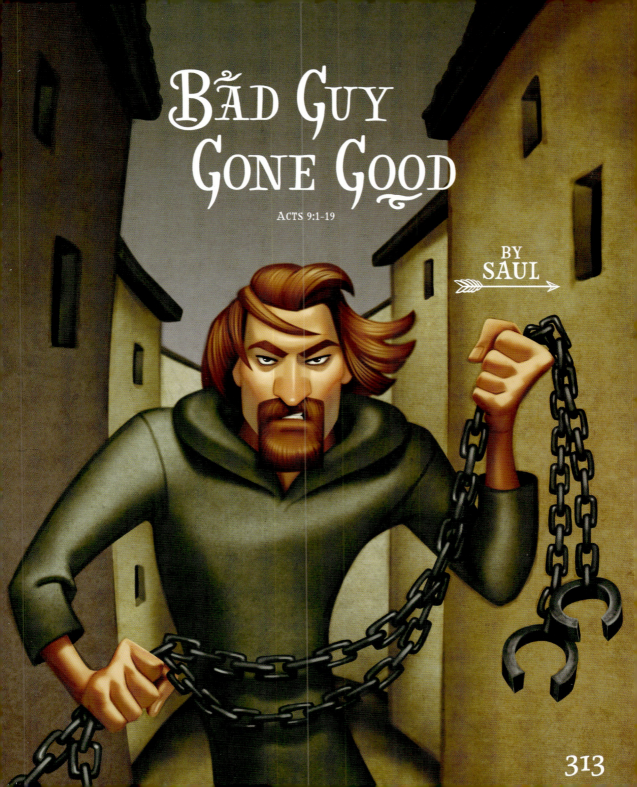

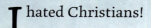

I hated Christians!

Jesus' followers made me mad. I hated them! They made me want to scream. If they weren't in jail or dead already, I was going to make sure they all got there one way or another.

But the last time I tried to hurt them, God got in my way.

I was on a mission. I'd been heading to Damascus to find more pesky Christians to put in jail. I planned to chain them up and make them pay for believing in Jesus. I couldn't wait to laugh when they cried in pain...oh, the anticipation!

But there I was, in the middle of the road, thinking about how many more Christians I could hurt when a blazing light flashed down from heaven right on top of me. It was so bright it drove me to my knees.

Then I heard a voice. "Saul! Saul! Why are you hurting me so much?"

"Who...who...who are you?" I called out, my jaw dropping to the ground.

"It's me, Jesus," said the voice. "And I'M the one you're hurting. I want you to go to the city, and then I'll tell you what to do next."

My friends who were with me were speechless and confused. They could hear the voice, too, but they couldn't see anyone else around. So strange! They helped me up and brushed me off.

But when I opened my eyes, I couldn't see a thing.

315

E VERYTHING in my life was changing fast.

My friends took me to a house in Damascus, and I sat there for three days. I was scared. I couldn't see. I couldn't eat. I couldn't drink.

Then God gave me a vision. He showed me that a man named Ananias would come and help me see again. Meanwhile, in another part of the city, Ananias wasn't so sure about that. He'd heard about me and how much I hated people like him who followed Jesus.

But God assured him I would be a changed man. And he was right. After this experience, I could never hurt another Christian again.

Sure enough, Ananias came to the house. Shaking, he laid his hands on me. Then a miracle happened! Something like scales fell off my eyes, and I could see again.

That's all it took for me to have a change of heart. I became a Christian, too, and I started becoming friends with other believers after that. *Hey, these Christians aren't so bad after all!* I told myself. My eyes had been opened in more ways than one.

If anyone tells you people can't change, just remember my story. I was lost, but then God found me. I was blind, but then God opened my eyes. I was unlovable, but God loved me.

Not only did my life change, but God even changed my name from Saul to Paul! I used to be Christians' worst enemy, but now I'm their biggest champion. And it's all because Jesus loved me and wanted me to be close to him. Now that I know God, I know Jesus is truly his Son.

Just like me, *you* can change, too. Is there anything in your life you'd like to change? Anything you'd like to stop doing? Maybe there's something good you'd like to start doing? Pray right now and ask God to change you.

≈ PAUL ≈

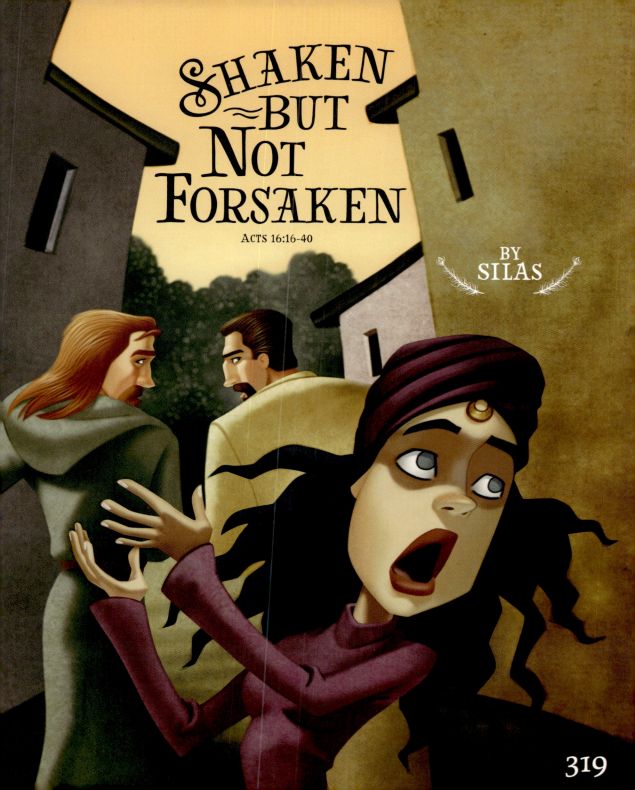

Shaken ≈ But Not Forsaken

Acts 16:16-40

BY SILAS

THE life of a missionary can be tough. We love the part where we tell everyone about Jesus. But Paul and I have been through a lot of tough stuff together. And the trouble we got into in Philippi was a *real* doozy.

The trouble started when we ran into a girl who was a fortuneteller. Her masters made quite a lot of money off of her abilities. They didn't know an evil spirit inside her helped her see the future.

Anyway, this girl started following us around and shouting to everyone, "These are men of God! They're here to tell you how to be saved!" That was great and all, but she kept shouting it, day after day after day.

Finally, Paul couldn't take it anymore. He turned around and, with God's power, told the nasty, evil spirit to leave the girl.

And it did.

Because of the power of Jesus, she was free!

But now her masters couldn't make money off her anymore. And they were *mad!*

THE girl's masters grabbed us off the street and dragged us to the city officials.

"These guys are troublemakers!" they yelled. "They're throwing the whole city into chaos because of their strange religion. And they're breaking the law!"

The mob turned on us fast. They beat us with big sticks and stole our clothes. It was all a blur. The next thing we knew, we were locked in a dungeon, bloodied and bruised, with our feet in shackles.

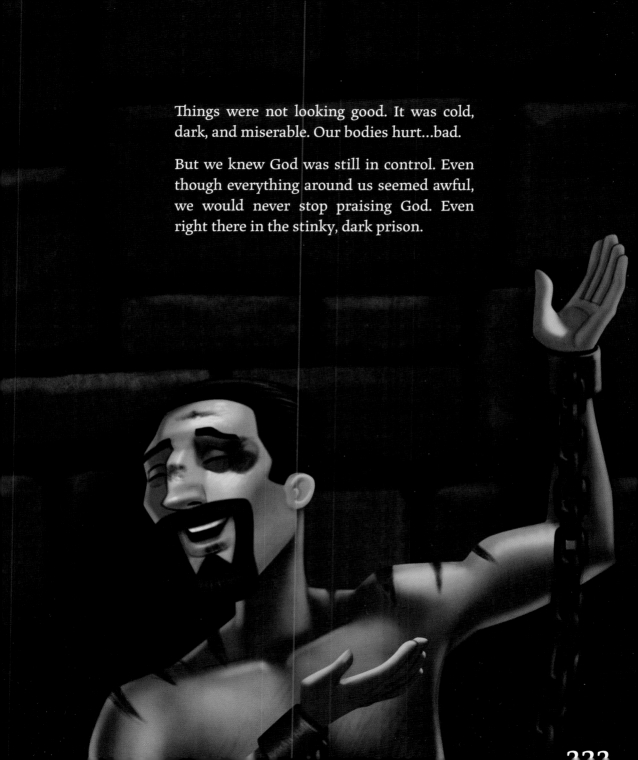

Things were not looking good. It was cold, dark, and miserable. Our bodies hurt...bad.

But we knew God was still in control. Even though everything around us seemed awful, we would never stop praising God. Even right there in the stinky, dark prison.

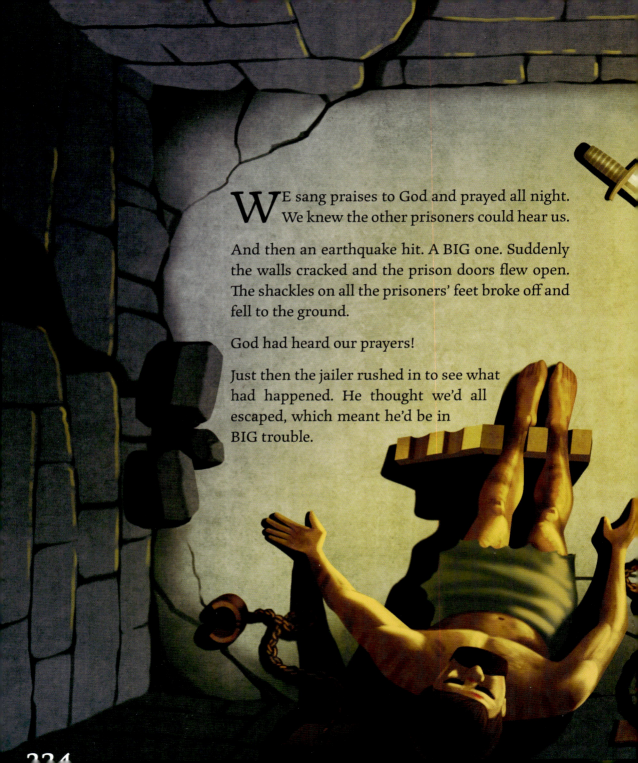

WE sang praises to God and prayed all night. We knew the other prisoners could hear us.

And then an earthquake hit. A BIG one. Suddenly the walls cracked and the prison doors flew open. The shackles on all the prisoners' feet broke off and fell to the ground.

God had heard our prayers!

Just then the jailer rushed in to see what had happened. He thought we'd all escaped, which meant he'd be in BIG trouble.

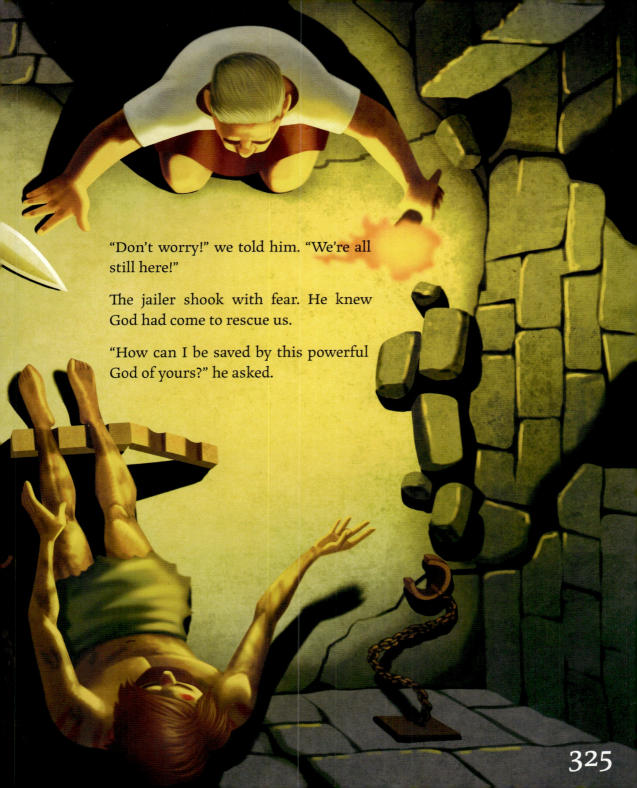

"Don't worry!" we told him. "We're all still here!"

The jailer shook with fear. He knew God had come to rescue us.

"How can I be saved by this powerful God of yours?" he asked.

WE told the jailer all about the good news of Jesus. His face lit up with hope.

Strange as it seems, he took us to his house and introduced us to his family. Even though it was the middle of the night, he cleaned us up and took care of our wounds. He even fed us some food.

I told the jailer that God loved him. "When you believe in Jesus, your whole family can be saved," I said.

The jailer and his family were overjoyed. They wanted to believe in Jesus, too!

The next morning the jailer learned the city officials had decided to set us free. They even told us they were sorry. Wow!

After that, we were able to keep on doing what we loved the most: telling more people about Jesus.

I'm not going to tell you that I like getting beaten up and thrown in dungeons. I don't like it one bit. It's terrible!

But I never forget that God is always in control. And better than that, God allowed Paul and me to go through that awful situation so we could help the jailer and his family know Jesus.

When bad things happen, it's hard to remember that God is still in control. We don't need to blame God. Instead, we can praise God, thank him, and pray for a way through the hard times. Who knows what plan God has in store!

What do *you* do when things get hard? Get angry? Go hide somewhere? Maybe cry a little? No matter what, just do what I did: pray. Maybe even sing a song. As always, God will be with you. And he might just surprise you with something *really* good!

 SILAS

My To-Do List for God

ACTS 16:1-4; 1 TIMOTHY 4:6-16;
6:11-21; 2 TIMOTHY 1:3-18

BY TIMOTHY

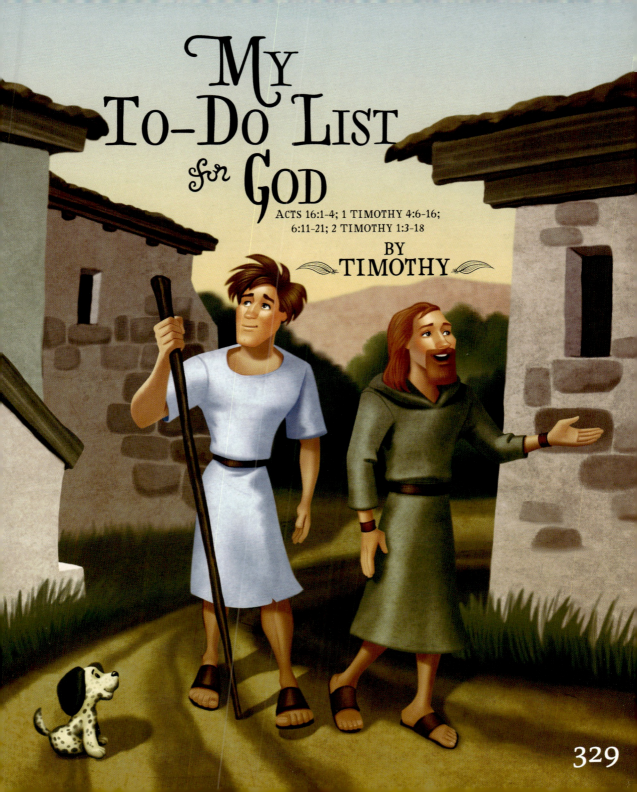

I'M pretty young for a missionary. When you're older, people tend to listen to you. But when you're young like me, people like to ignore you. You know what I mean?

But Paul believed in me. He knew how much I loved Jesus. So Paul asked me to go with him on one of his missionary journeys. We went from town to town, telling people about Jesus' love. It was great! I learned a lot about God while we were together, and I cried when it was over.

Later, Paul ended up in prison. While he was there, he wrote me a couple of letters. He gave me a lot of great advice for helping me live a life that makes God happy. I call it my "To-Do List for God."

- It's good to keep your body healthy, but it's even better to keep your spirit healthy.

- Let the words of Jesus be the most important food you eat.

- Even though you're young, you can still be a great example for how to love others.

- Don't waste your time arguing with people; it's not worth it.

- Always keep your hope in God, and nothing else.

- God has given you a gift, so use it every chance you get.

- Stay true to what is right.

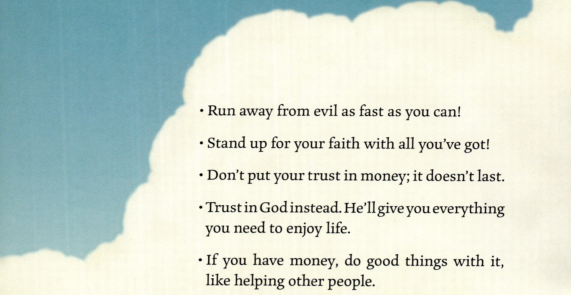

- Run away from evil as fast as you can!

- Stand up for your faith with all you've got!

- Don't put your trust in money; it doesn't last.

- Trust in God instead. He'll give you everything you need to enjoy life.

- If you have money, do good things with it, like helping other people.

- Tell people everything you know about Jesus.

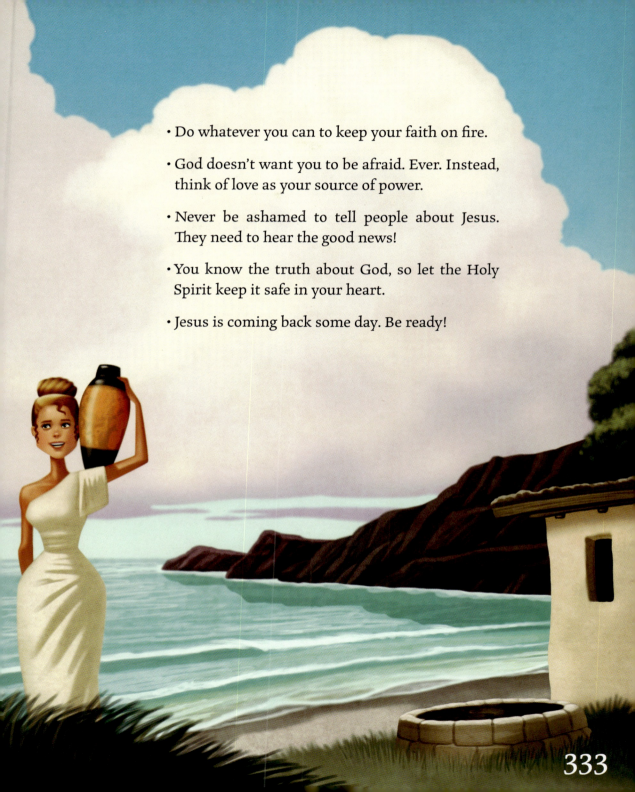

- Do whatever you can to keep your faith on fire.

- God doesn't want you to be afraid. Ever. Instead, think of love as your source of power.

- Never be ashamed to tell people about Jesus. They need to hear the good news!

- You know the truth about God, so let the Holy Spirit keep it safe in your heart.

- Jesus is coming back some day. Be ready!

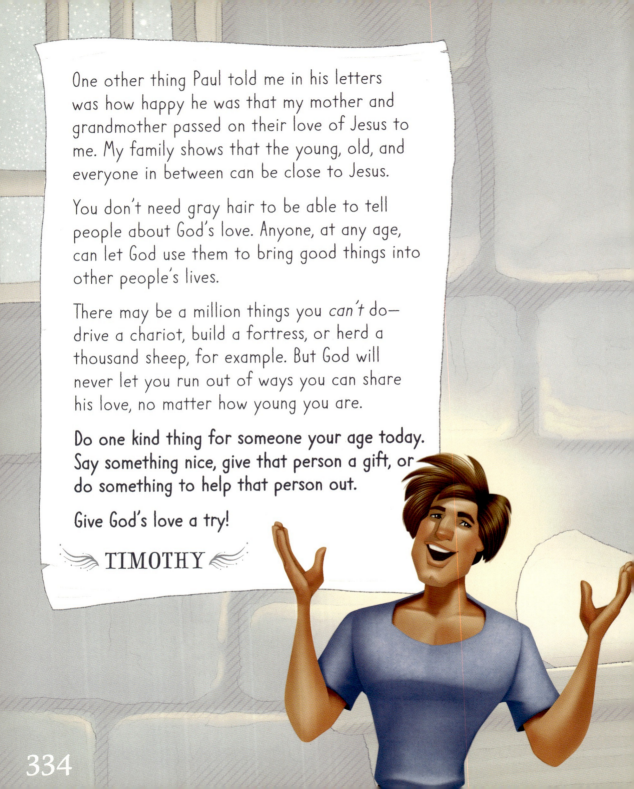

One other thing Paul told me in his letters was how happy he was that my mother and grandmother passed on their love of Jesus to me. My family shows that the young, old, and everyone in between can be close to Jesus.

You don't need gray hair to be able to tell people about God's love. Anyone, at any age, can let God use them to bring good things into other people's lives.

There may be a million things you *can't* do—drive a chariot, build a fortress, or herd a thousand sheep, for example. But God will never let you run out of ways you can share his love, no matter how young you are.

Do one kind thing for someone your age today. Say something nice, give that person a gift, or do something to help that person out.

Give God's love a try!

⤙ TIMOTHY ⤚

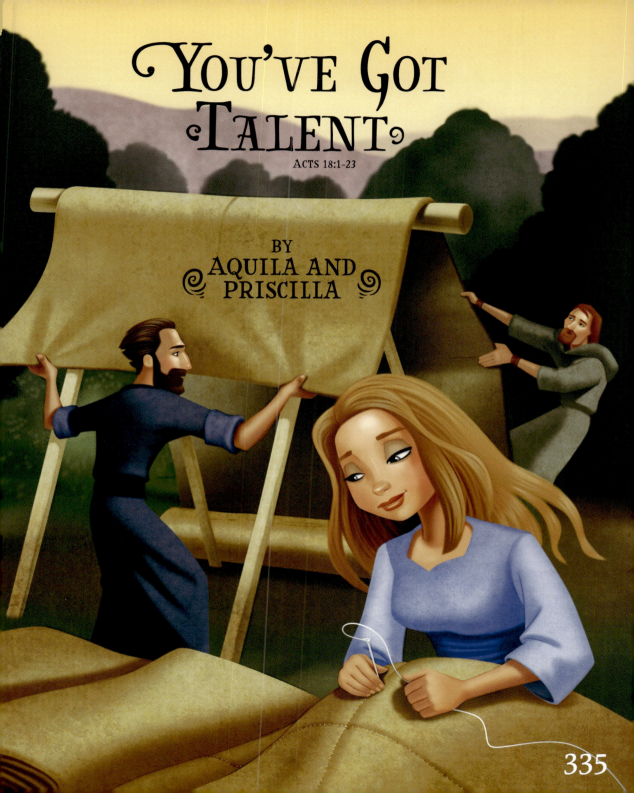

You've Got Talent

ACTS 18:1-23

BY
AQUILA AND PRISCILLA

THERE'S nothing wrong with a bit of good, hard work. We should know, because we make tents. Some people are carpenters, some go fishing, and others paint for a living. But we're tentmakers. It's good work for a married couple like us, and everybody has to have a tent, right?

But making tents was just a job. Our real work was for God. We wanted everyone to know about Jesus.

It made us especially happy when Paul came and started working with us. He was a tentmaker, too, you know. And he was very good at talking to people about Jesus. In fact, every Sabbath day we'd go with Paul to the local Jewish church where he would try to convince people to believe in Jesus.

Some people loved what Paul had to say, but others didn't want to hear it. One time they got so mad at Paul they dragged him to court to try to get him put in jail.

(Thankfully, the judge thought they were being ridiculous and told them all to leave.)

ONE of the best things we learned from Paul was something God told him in a vision one night:

"Don't be silent! Don't be afraid to say what you need to say. I'm always with you, and I won't let anyone hurt you," God told him.

That was exactly what we needed to hear. Even though some people didn't like us talking about Jesus all the time, God kept us safe and allowed us to keep sharing the good news.

We liked working with Paul. We also loved being able to do our jobs—making tents AND telling people about Jesus. So we decided to stick with Paul for a while.

We even sailed away with Paul to other cities, using our tents and talents for God in every way we could.

A tent is a place you live in. We all need a place where our bodies can rest and be safe.

But your heart needs a different kind of shelter. Your heart needs to live with God. God is the only one who can fill your heart with love—so much love that you can share it with other people.

When we're close to God, we can use our talents to do good things for him. ANYBODY can serve God, no matter what he or she does. Whether someone is a cook, an athlete, a soldier, a doctor, or a student, God has given every person skills that can be used to share Jesus' love.

What's one thing *you're* really good at? How can you use that talent in a way that serves God?

⛺ AQUILA AND PRISCILLA ⛺

The End That's Also the Beginning

REVELATION 21–22

BY ❧ JOHN ❧

I'VE seen the future, and I think you're going to love it.

God gave me a peek at what it will be like when everything as we know it will come to an end, and God will create a whole new world for us. (God said I could tell you about it, by the way.)

This new world will blow you away. Its capital city will be called the new Jerusalem, and it's going to be HUGE. The whole thing will be made of gold, as clear as glass. It'll be surrounded by angels guarding a giant wall. Each of the twelve gates will be made from a single pearl!

In the city God and Jesus will sit on a throne, and they'll shine brighter than anything you've ever seen. We won't even need the sun anymore! And from the throne will flow a river with the water of life, as clear as crystal. Trees of life will grow on both sides of the river, bearing fruit that never runs out.

Best of all, God and Jesus will live there! And WE will be their friends, their neighbors!

It'll be the most perfect place you could imagine. No more tears, no more pain, no more nighttime, no more dying, and not a hint of evil anywhere.

ONLY those who love Jesus will be allowed in God's city. Only those who are thirsty for God can live there.

And we, his children, will finally be able to see God's face! We'll worship God like we've never worshipped him before.

AWESOME!

When I saw this vision, I was overcome with joy. The thought of living forever with God and his Son, Jesus, made my heart feel like it would burst!

All we're waiting for now is Jesus to come back.

Jesus was there when our world started, and he'll be here when it stops. He said it best himself: "I am the Alpha and the Omega, the First and the Last, the Beginning and the End."

For now, we listen. We wait for Jesus. We keep our eyes and ears open. Because one day soon, we'll all hear God's Spirit say, once and for all, "Come."

Amen.

So here we are. It's been quite a journey, hasn't it? Miracles, wonders, defeats, and victories. And, as God's vision showed me, an amazing future to look forward to.

But this story isn't over yet.

YOU are as much a part of God's story as any of us: Adam, Eve, Abraham, Moses, Rahab, Esther—and me, John. We were just getting things started. We each had a special friendship with God.

Now it's your turn.

God wants a friendship with you, too. Jesus wants to be with you forever. When you believe in him, someday you can live with God in that spectacular city of gold, too!

But right now *you* have your part in God's story. Now is your turn to share God's love with the people in your life. Now is the time for you to show the world how everyone can be God's friend, too. You can tell people about Jesus!

So, go.

You're never alone.
You can do it!

 JOHN

YOUR
STORY

BY
YOU!

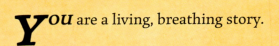

You are a living, breathing story.

Like he did for Adam and Eve, God has given you the gift of life...and the freedom to choose right or wrong. Like Joseph, your life will have countless ups and downs...and a purpose you might not yet understand. Like Thomas, you may have doubts from time to time, but Jesus can use your doubts to make your faith even stronger.

And through it all, God will be right by your side.

There's a verse in the Bible that says this: "So now we can rejoice in our wonderful new relationship with God because our Lord Jesus Christ has made us **friends of God**" (Romans 5:11).

That's right. Jesus made it possible for YOU to be God's friend.

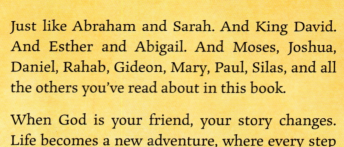

Just like Abraham and Sarah. And King David. And Esther and Abigail. And Moses, Joshua, Daniel, Rahab, Gideon, Mary, Paul, Silas, and all the others you've read about in this book.

When God is your friend, your story changes. Life becomes a new adventure, where every step you take is a chance to experience God's love and share it with others. Where you start to see God at work all around you. Where God can surprise you with gifts that make you mightier than you ever thought possible.

It all starts with Jesus. Because of his great love, his story can be *your* story. His joy can be *your* joy. And his power can be *your* power.

Your life is the pen, God's love is the ink, and the world is your paper.

What will *your* story be?

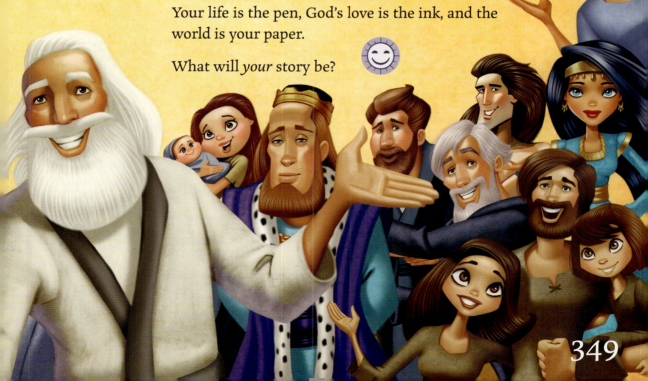

349

MY FAVORITE PARTS OF THE BIBLE:

JEFF White is a lead content developer for Group Publishing, where he's written or co-written 15 books for church ministry and faith development. He has a passion for helping people grow their creativity, and leads creativity workshops at ministry conferences around the country. A graduate of Biola University, Jeff has also published several books for young readers, including *The Runaway Candy Cane.*

DAVID Harrington's love for art began at an early age when he drew on everything, which eventually lead to a career in illustration. He graduated from the Art Center College of Design in Pasadena, where he earned a bachelor's degree in fine arts with honors. David has illustrated numerous children's books and enjoys snowboarding, surfing, and spending time with his wife and children in Laguna Hills, California.